PROPHESY!

A Practical Guide To
Developing Your
Prophetic Gift

BRUCE COLLINS

First Published in Great Britain in 2000 by **New Wine International Publishing**.
New Edition Published in 2003 by Kingsway Communications Ltd England

This Edition Published in 2006 by **New Wine Resources**
4a Ridley Avenue, Ealing, London W13 9XW, England
ISBN 1 902977 06 8

Typeset & cover design by The Design Chapel
Printed in Great Britain by Biddles Ltd.

**This book is dedicated
to two Davids.**

To David Parker,
for teaching me much of what I have
learnt about prophecy.

To David Pytches,
for providing me with so many opportunities
to teach this to others.

Scripture tells us to 'eagerly desire the spiritual gifts especially the gift of prophecy'. I have known Bruce for many years. He has that necessary combination of being a solid and perceptive Bible teacher, a practitioner in prophetic ministry and an amazing trainer of others. This book is full of insightful teaching and practical wisdom for all those who long to grow in the prophetic and encourage its use in the local church. I highly commend it.

Mike Pilavachi - Leader of Soul Survivor UK

I first learnt about the practice of New Testament prophecy in the church from Bruce. My appreciation of the value of using this gift to build up the Church has grown since then. The Church needs to rediscover this tool which God has given to connect his people to Him and release them further into His purposes. This gift grows leaders who practise it and those who receive encouragement and strength from hearing God. I commend this book warmly.

Ven. Nigel Juckes - St. Agnes, Kloof, South Africa

Have you knocked at the back of too many wardrobes lately and walked away with a sigh of disappointment? You know the world of prophecy is real, you have obeyed the biblical command to earnestly desire this gift but you cannot get into it. In your hands you are holding right now something that is not meant to exist. It is a door into another world that will work every time for anyone who reads its clear teaching and follows the practical guidelines it sets out. Don't be deceived, this book may look thin as you hold it in your hands, but it is like the Tardis be you a beginner or a more seasoned prophetic traveller, or a church leader looking for a proven and well defined track that is safe for sheep to walk on and leads to good pastures! Open it's door and go in and enjoy adventures in God for years to come. It is my prayer that out of this happy marriage of Word and Spirit, healthy prophetic ministry can be born that will bless your life and indeed bless and enrich the life of many Churches.

Kenny Borthwick - Leader, Clan Gathering, Scotland

In our fast changing world it is crucial that the Church rediscovers the content and dynamics of the Apostolic faith. Bruce Collins not only practises, but also teaches and trains Christians all over the world in the use of the gift of prophecy. This book can change your ministry so that it draws people's attention to the New Testament Gospel that comes not only in words but also in power.

Kjell Axel Johanson - Senior Pastor, Elimkyrkan, Stockholm, Sweden

Bruce has condensed a lot of his teaching in this fine practical book. Specially useful for Church leaders who want to lead their congregation into hearing God and speaking words of encouragement that God wants spoken to his people through the ministry of others. It has been a blessing to us and I hope it will be for many others.

Dick Westerkamp - Dominee, Nederlands Gereformeerde Kerk,
Houten, Holland

CONTENTS

FOREWORD

"Bruce Collins, a Church leader experienced in renewal, with a proven prophetic gift himself, has written this excellent book, 'Prophesy!'. It is one of the clearest and most practical books on the subject I have seen, and I hope as many people as possible will read it.

Paul, the Apostle, wrote to the Corinthian Church and urged the Christians there to pursue prophecy as a really useful gift for building up the Church. In 1 Corinthians 14 he tells them twice to "be eager to prophesy."

Too many of us have not got a clue what it is, how and when to use it, and how to test it. Bruce takes it all in his stride and spells these things out for us in a most helpful way.

I warmly commend this very practical handbook not only for all would-be prophets, but for any Christian who wants to grow in hearing the Lord more clearly.

I also commend it to Church leaders. Use it in your home groups or other settings as a practical course to sow prophecy into your Church!"

David Pytches

ACKNOWLEDGEMENTS

I want to express my heartfelt thanks to -

My Bishop, Graham Dow, the Bishop of Willesden, who has been a wonderful source of encouragement to me in my ministry as it has developed in recent years.

The Roxeth Team Ministry in Harrow which has been so generous in supporting the wider faith-sharing work I and others have taken out from Harrow.

The Trustees and leaders of New Wine, and others who have given generous support and encouragement over these last years.

Richard Scott, Loraine Craig, Freda Meadows, Angela Bamping and others who have come out on team with me, heard me teach about prophecy many times, and have themselves blessed and helped so many people through their prophetic ministries and personal examples.

My wife Siân, sons Tom and Matthew, and daughter Kate, without whose love, encouragement, prayer - and forbearance of my regular absence on trips, I could not do the work I do.

Bruce Collins *May 2000*

INTRODUCTION

Despite a long background of Christian worship at Church Schools and local Anglican Churches, I only came to experience charismatic gifts like prophecy being expressed in gatherings in 1979 at an Anglican Church in Cricklewood, in London. Initially I wasn't very impressed! Some in the Church were very broken people, and I soon learnt much about how the gift of prophecy can be mishandled by some! And amidst some quite accurate or striking 'words', there were others which didn't seem to strike me as coming from God, and appeared to be rather more like 'worthy thoughts' than communication direct from heaven.

But later I came to have first hand experience of the Lord speaking to me through prophecies from gifted and mature Christians. I also came to see this gift being responsibly taught and handled in a Church by leaders like David Pytches in St. Andrews, Chorleywood. This quickly aroused a hunger in me to grow in this gift for myself.

Later I was given much encouragement through the teaching and ministry of David Parker, a senior Vineyard Pastor, when he was over here in the UK. The personal ministry he gave to me, and the way he took trouble to encourage me by taking me out with him to help on visits to other Churches and leaders' gatherings was an enormous help. Through this, David taught me much about how we can help and empower one another to grow in the kind of faith that we need in order to grow in prophecy and other gifts of the Holy Spirit.

Since then I have had the privilege of teaching prophecy at New Wine, and at Churches and conferences in many places. It has been a great joy to see literally thousands of Christians discover how easy it is to start using this lovely gift, and how much blessing it can bring to people or Churches when it is responsibly and lovingly exercised.

This book does not attempt to be a comprehensive handbook on prophecy. I am not competent to write such a book, and others have done so. Instead I have tried to set out in a simple, readable way, the teaching I have given in many places to help people begin to prophesy and then grow in their prophetic gifting. I also try to give some practical guidance on how prophecy can be responsibly handled and cultivated in the local Church.

I hope it will be a helpful tool for Church leaders who want to train their people to use the gift of prophecy, and for individual Christians who want to develop their prophetic gifting.

My prayer is that the Lord will help all his Church to recover a Biblical understanding of this wonderful, and very powerful gift, and that its mature expression will become commonplace in most Churches.

CHAPTER ONE

WHY IS PROPHECY IMPORTANT?

If we don't see why we need something, or appreciate its value to us, we won't hunger for it. This is why I want to begin this book by seeking to show why prophecy is so valuable for the Church.

Why then is prophecy important!

First, and most important - because the Bible says it is! In his first letter to the Corinthians Paul tells us to 'Follow the way of love and eagerly desire spiritual gifts, especially the gift of prophecy.' (1Cor 14:1) he clearly saw this as the premier gift of the Holy Spirit.

We also see the priority of prophetic *ministry* two chapters earlier, when he writes about different ministries within the body of Christ. Paul writes 'And in the Church God has appointed first of all apostles, second prophets...' and then he lists teachers, workers of miracles, and other important ministries within the life of the Church (1 Cor 12:28). In a similar list in his letter to the Ephesian Church (Eph 4:11) we find that there too he lists those gifted to exercise prophetic ministries immediately after those with apostolic gifting.

As one who believes that the Bible is the inspired and authoritative word of God, I would have anticipated seeing Paul list the gift of teacher in this second position. But teachers need to know what the Lord might want taught to his Church at a given time! It is through apostolic leadership and the influence of those with prophetic ministries that they will be helped to know what needs to be taught, and I think this is one example of why Paul gives prophetic ministry an earlier priority.

It is also interesting to see that Old Testament prophecies about life for God's people in the New Covenant, following the coming of Christ and the outpouring of the Holy Spirit, show that the key *sign* of this outpouring of the Spirit would be prophecy. So, Joel prophesied 'And afterwards, (the Lord says), I will pour out my Spirit on all people. Your sons and daughters will prophesy, your old men will dream dreams, your young men will see visions.' (Joel 2.28).

This was fulfilled on the day of Pentecost when the Lord first poured out his Spirit on the Church. Although the disciples were inspired by the Holy Spirit to speak in languages which they themselves did not understand, these proved to be prophetic utterances in the wide variety of languages used by those who

4

gathered around them. So this was in effect a powerful, *supernatural* confirmation to their hearers that the Holy Spirit had come upon the Church.

Prophecy is *usually* the key sign of the outpouring of the Spirit upon people in the Bible. When Moses prayed for the Spirit to come upon the elders of the people of Israel in the wilderness they prophesied. (Num 11:25) Two of the elders, Eldad and Medad, had remained in the camp and yet the Spirit also rested on them and they prophesied too, (v26). A young man then ran and told Moses what was happening, and Joshua spoke up and said 'Moses, my Lord, stop them!'. But Moses replied 'Are you jealous for my sake? I wish that all the Lord's people were prophets and that the Lord would put his Spirit on them!' (v29).

Moses longed to see the Holy Spirit come on all the people of God so that they would truly be a prophetic people. This is the reality that God has made possible in the New Covenant, where all his people can be filled with the Holy Spirit. (Ez 36:26,27, Jn 1:33, 7:38,39, etc.)

God has always regarded his people in this way. As Psalm 105 shows, this is the way he even regarded his old covenant people when they were wandering through the wilderness. In verse 14 we read that 'He allowed no-one to oppress them; for their sake he rebuked kings.' And then in verse 15 God says 'Do not touch my anointed ones, do my prophets no harm'.

In the New Covenant his people are called 'Christians'. This literally means 'little anointed ones', and as I will show later, this means that we can all exercise the gift of prophecy.

But why is it so important that we are a prophetic people!

To answer this important question we must go back to the very beginning of the Bible.

In the Old Testament

When God created human beings, he said 'Let us make man in our image, in our likeness, and let them rule over the fish of the sea and the birds of the air, over the livestock and over all the earth, and over all the creatures that move along the ground.' (Gn1:26) In verse 28 we read of him blessing man and woman and saying to them 'Be fruitful and increase in number; fill the earth and subdue it. Rule over the fish of the sea and the birds of the air and over every living creature that moves on the ground.'

So when he created us, it is clear that God entrusted human beings with responsibility for the exercise of his Kingdom over the world.

We see this same truth clearly set out for us in Psalm 8, a creation psalm which first rejoices over the majesty of God's glory reflected in the created order. It then goes on to consider who man is in God's sight and purposes. In verses 3 to 8 we read 'When I consider your heavens, the work of your fingers, the moon and the stars, which you have set in place, what is man that you are mindful of him, the son of man that you care for him? You made him a little lower than the heavenly beings and crowned him with glory and honour. You made him ruler over the works of your hands; you put everything under his feet: all flocks and herds, and the beasts of the field, the birds of the air, and the fish of the sea, all that swim the paths of the seas.'

In other words, we were created in God's image and likeness first so that we could enjoy living, personal relationship with him, and then through that relationship, to be responsible for the exercise of his Kingdom on earth. This is why Jesus teaches his New Covenant people to pray 'Our Father in heaven.... your kingdom come, your will be done on earth as it is in heaven.' (Matt 6:10) And for all this to be possible, he breathed his breath (Spirit) into us, so creating us to be spiritual beings, able to draw on the Holy Spirit's resources to fulfil our calling. This meant that we would be able to hear his voice, see what he wanted to reveal to us, and find his guidance for our expression of his Kingdom in the world.

This truth is repeated in another Psalm which says 'The highest heavens belong to the Lord, but the earth he has given to man' (Ps 115:16).

This is the way God always meant it to be! Just as he created the world we live in through his Word and by his Spirit, so as we listen to what he tells us, and step out to do it in his Name, he gives us his Holy Spirit to enable us to fulfil what he has spoken. ('Not by might, nor by power, but by my Spirit says the Lord Almighty.' (Zech 4:6)).

So hearing God is a central key to releasing the presence, gifts and power (i.e. 'anointing') of God on what we do in his Name. This is what the Church needs more than anything else!

In the New Testament

These truths are exactly what Jesus taught us in John's Gospel, where he describes himself as the Good Shepherd who leads his sheep through his voice. (Jn10) In verse 3 he perfectly describes the role and purpose of prophetic *ministry* in the church. 'The watchman opens the gate for him, and the sheep listen to his voice.'

This is always the role of the watchmen and women in the Church. Their role is to watch to see what the Lord is doing, and to hear what he is saying so that the Church is helped to be more closely connected to the Lord and his purposes for them.

Jesus described John the Baptist as the greatest of the Old Testament prophets ('watchmen'). And this is precisely what John's ministry accomplished. He 'prepared the way of the Lord' and opened the gate for Jesus to be recognised by many of his people when he came to live in Israel 2000 years ago.

But we all need to hear his voice! Jesus said that he '.... calls his own sheep by name and leads them out.' (Jn 10:3b). This is how we first come to know the Lord. We first truly commit our lives to him when we hear him speaking personally to us, revealing his personal love for us, his forgiveness of our sins, and how much he longs to live in intimate communion with us. 'Here I am! I stand at the door *(of your life)* and knock. If anyone hears my voice and opens the door, I will come in and eat with him, and he with me.' (Rev 3:20 - my amplification in italics).

The point here is that the door is closed when he knocks on it, and it is when we hear his voice and respond by faith, opening the door to him, that we come to know him and experience intimacy with him. And from then on he continues to lead us by speaking to us. (Jn 10:3,4)

The same is true of our corporate discipleship as whole Churches. In John 10:4 Jesus said 'When he has brought out all his own, he goes on ahead of them, and his sheep follow him because they *(collectively)* know his voice.' (My amplification in italics). So a critical question for our Churches is: How good are we at hearing the Lord's voice together? How often do we ask one another the question 'What is the Lord saying to us in our present circumstances?' or 'What is the Lord saying to us through the problems or difficulties we are facing right now?' Do we have a Church culture in which it is common to hear people speaking (humbly!) about what they feel the Lord *may* have said to them?

In Conclusion

This theme of the Lord leading his people by speaking to them runs right through the Bible.

In the book of Amos we are told 'Surely the Sovereign Lord does *nothing* without revealing his plans to his servants the prophets.' (Amos 3:7 - my italics). In Isaiah we read of God saying 'See, the former things have taken place, and new things I declare; before they spring into being I announce them to you' (Isa 42:9).

Earlier in Isaiah we see God taking his Old Testament people to task because they were consulting mediums and spiritists, and asking of them why they did not instead 'inquire of their God?'

(Isa 8:19) And later in Isaiah, when God calls his people to cry to him in prayer for help, one of his promises if they responded to this call was 'Whether you turn to the right or to the left, your ears will hear a voice behind you, saying "This is the way; walk in it".' (Isa 30:21) In other words God is here again promising to lead his people by his voice.

So the central purpose of prophecy is always to connect us to the Lord, his heart, purposes and plans for us, and to help us better fulfil his Kingdom purposes for our lives and the lives of our churches.

This is exactly what we are told in the Book of Revelation, where the angel says to the apostle John '... the testimony of Jesus is the spirit of prophecy' (Rev19:10). Sometimes the word 'spirit' in the New Testament refers to the spirit of a person or the Spirit of the Lord, but here it's meaning is the word 'essence'. In other words the essence of what prophecy does is to reveal ('testify to') Jesus - who he is, his heart and love for us, and his desire to encourage and envision us as we seek to serve him.

While knowing Jesus personally is the most important reality of all, there are surely few other things more important than being directly connected to his heart and purposes for our lives. Prophecy is important!

But Isaiah helps us to see one more very important thing about the power of prophecy. In Isaiah 55, the Lord calls his people to listen to him and come near to him to hear his voice. Then he goes on to say 'As the rain and the snow come down from heaven, and do not return to it without watering the earth and making it bud and flourish, so that it yields seed for the sower and bread for the eater, so is my word that goes out from my mouth: It will not return to me empty, but will accomplish what I desire and achieve the purpose for which I sent it'. (Isa 55:10,11).

This is a wonderful promise! If we rightly hear and weigh what the Lord says to us about his purposes for our church or our circumstances, and then by faith start speaking this 'word' to others around us, *that word itself has God's living power in it to bring into existence something that doesn't as yet exist,* because God's Spirit always creates what his Word speaks. And even if those around us find it difficult to believe this 'word', if we truly have heard the Lord and are speaking it appropriately under his guidance, we can trust him to honour and fulfil it!

I have seen the truth of this many times now. The Lord has spoken to me and others about all the key developments in the Churches I have led since ordination, and in more recent years about the wider ministry it seems he has given me to do. Each time I found these prophecies all but impossible to believe when they first came, but as I and others talked and prayed about them, we have seen him bring about what he has called us to speak in his Name.

He's wonderful! *Ask* him to speak to you or your Church and wait on him in expectancy until he answers, pray for fulfilment of what you sincerely believe he has spoken, and then speak and work with him for its fulfilment. It is truly exciting to work with him like this.

CHAPTER TWO

DIFFERENT WAYS PROPHECY BRINGS BLESSING

In his first letter to the Corinthian Church Paul teaches us that those who prophesy speak to people for their '...strengthening, encouragement and comfort.' (1 Cor 14:3) Later in that chapter he teaches that we can all prophesy in turn so that everybody may be instructed and encouraged (1Cor 14:31). Over the years I have come to see how the Lord can use this wonderful gift in many different ways to bring his blessing and help to people.

1.Communicating Grace, Peace and Comfort

True prophecy usually communicates the Lord's grace and peace to people. Paul opens all his letters (which are directly inspired by God) with the greeting 'Grace and peace to you from God our Father and the Lord Jesus Christ'. It is particularly interesting to see that in both letters to Timothy he adds an additional word to the opening greeting 'Grace, *mercy* and peace to you from God our Father and Christ Jesus our Lord'.

The first time I experienced prophecy bringing mercy and comfort to me happened in 1982, when I was at a small conference for leaders. We were sitting in silence on the first morning after some deep worship. Far from feeling uplifted by this, I was self-preoccupied and in much emotional pain. Only two nights previously I had had a serious row with someone close to me. It had been entirely my own fault, and I was feeling very guilty and ashamed about this.

Then a mature Christian woman spoke: 'I believe that the Lord is showing me that there is a man here who had a row with someone two nights ago and this is what I believe he wants to say to you...' It was as though the Lord came and stood directly in front of me and through her, spoke words of mercy and forgiveness, correction and encouragement to me.

I was astounded, and profoundly touched that he could be so direct and gracious to me! In consequence I knew I wanted to love Jesus more than ever before. Second, I wanted to get to the person I had hurt as soon as opportunity provided to ask forgiveness and make amends, and third, I was now released to enter into all the good things that the Lord had for me and the others at that conference. And all this happened simply because of the faith and openness to the Lord of another Christian there.

Now I know that we all need to learn to grow strong in the Lord's grace declared to us in the Bible, and to deal appropriately with these times of sin and failure by learning to stand firmly in the truth of the gospel. But nevertheless I have found that I am not alone in sometimes needing special help from the Lord through others around me to overcome times of despondency like that.

I also find myself wondering how many times the Lord might have wanted to use us to provide similar comfort and help to others who might be in much private pain when they come to our Sunday morning services, or who we meet on other occasions.

2. Encouragement

Time and again I have seen the Lord give amazing encouragement to people through gifts of prophecy.

On one occasion I was offering personal prophetic ministry in a group setting to a man who I had never met before. As I looked at him and asked the Lord to give me a word that would bring him encouragement, suddenly a strange thought came into my mind. 'Tell him I like the way he drinks his beer!' I immediately dismissed this as some irrational thought of my own, and so I waited longer, asking the Lord to give me a true word of prophecy to help him.

Nothing else seemed to come, but this strange thought kept on coming back into my mind. So eventually I said to him 'This seems most unlike a prophecy to me, and please ignore it if it doesn't make sense to you, but if it is the Lord I think he is telling me that he likes the way you drink your beer!' At this point the man appeared totally astonished, and the rest of the group who heard it almost fell off their chairs laughing.

It turned out that only two weeks before, he had told others in the Church that he sincerely believed the Lord had spoken to him and called him to go and share the gospel with men in a local pub! So he had begun to do this and had found it rather difficult. This had led him to doubt whether he had really heard the Lord in the first place. So my word gave him immense encouragement, because it reaffirmed that he had heard the Lord correctly, and that he was with him there in the pub as he sought to create openings for the gospel with these men.

In 1991 David Parker, a Vineyard Pastor from the United States, came to do a series of teaching evenings on prophecy at our churches in Harrow. One of the things he taught us about prophecy was it's power to release people from what he called 'cages of discouragement'.

He explained that there are many Christians who at some time in their lives have dared to believe that the Lord intended to use them or their churches for a bigger faith venture. But because later on this venture did not work out too well, they then allowed themselves to be locked into a 'cage' of discouragement. They had believed the lie that they dare not expect God to use them in some more significant way in the future. He might do wonderful things through other Christians or their Churches but not with them. David showed how powerfully a prophetic word can enter such 'cages' to break the power of these lies.

I first saw this happen when soon afterwards David invited me to go out with him when he was speaking at meetings in Kent. He encouraged me to seek the Lord for prophetic words for individuals at these meetings while he was speaking. I had never done this before, and so I was very doubtful that anything would come to me at all!

At the first of these meetings I sensed the Lord pointing out an ordained lady to me. As I looked at her and prayed, I was surprised to find a number of thoughts and impressions coming to my mind and so I wrote these down. I then found the Lord giving me words for a few other people at the meeting and as they seemed to be leaving first at the end of the meeting I spoke those to them first.

By the time I came to give what I felt I'd received for the first lady, I found that David Parker was already talking with her. But he suddenly looked round and said to me 'Bruce you have a word for her don't you?', and asked me to come and give them to her. As I spoke to her two things happened. She started weeping and David started laughing! When I finished, speaking I was very curious to find out why this was so.

David explained to me that about two years previously he had met her and given her prophetic words. However, she was serving in a Church that did not encourage the use of the gifts of the Holy Spirit or some of the dimensions of ministry that David had prophesied about to her. She had therefore become very discouraged, and had started to believe that what David had spoken to her was not truly from the Lord. David then went on to explain that the reason the words I had spoken to her had had such impact on her was that they were virtually identical to the things he had spoken to her two years previously! She was enormously encouraged, and has since gone on from strength to strength in those dimensions of her ministry.

But I have to say I was hugely encouraged too. The fact that I had heard something similar to what David, someone so mature in prophetic ministry had heard was encouragement enough for me!

The Lord really loves to encourage his people, and especially when we are facing important decisions. A couple of years ago some of us made a visit to New Zealand. On the first evening of a conference on South Island, one of the team pointed to a man there and said 'I believe the Lord is calling you into significant leadership in his Church'. The man was visibly astonished. We later learned that about two years previously he had believed that the Lord might be calling him into the ordained ministry. Because he had had many doubts about this he had put this call to one side. But only a couple of weeks before the conference he had sensed a fresh stirring of this call, and so he had asked the Lord to give him some clear, unsolicited confirmation that this call was truly from him!

The fact that this word came from a complete stranger who knew nothing about these things, and was in fact the first prophetic word to be given out at the conference, helped him enormously. But I must stress here that even a prophecy like this did not *prove* that the Lord was calling him to ordained leadership, even if it seemed to be a clear signpost to him to seek the Lord about this with fresh faith and expectancy. All prophecy must be weighed.

3. Discernment of Gifting

Paul once wrote to Timothy 'Do not neglect your gift, which was given you through a prophetic message when the body of elders laid their hands on you'. (1 Tim 4:14)

I have found that the Lord loves to use a gift of prophecy to identify or confirm the ministry giftings that he has already given to his people. The Church is the body of Christ, so it stands to reason that the sooner we can discern the ministry, calling and gifting that God has given to each of his people (and especially those who are new in the Christian faith), the sooner we can help them to be trained, equipped and released into those ministries.

People usually love operating in their spiritual gifting, because this is one of the most direct ways in which we can be aware of consciously working in partnership with the Holy Spirit. So we also grow more rapidly in our walk with the Lord and in our ministries if we know how He has gifted and called us and are given opportunities to exercise that gifting.

There are other ways in which we can grow to discern how God has gifted and called people, but often prophecy enables us to identify these things in a person long before they might be discerned by natural means.

Whenever I seek the Lord in prayer for people, I almost always ask him to show me how he has called and gifted them for ministry. Apart from any other revelation that the Lord might give, this always brings encouragement to people as the Lord affirms them in the gifts and calling they are already aware of. I think this is part of what Paul means when he uses the word 'strengthen' in 1 Corinthians 14:3. It is only possible to strengthen something that already exists, and people usually desire to do things for which they sense they are gifted.

4. Guidance for the church and its leaders

When Paul writes about the Church as the body of Christ in his first letter to the Corinthian Church, he wrote 'And in the Church God has appointed first of all apostles, second prophets, third teachers, then workers of miracles,...' (1Cor12:28).

This is not an exhaustive list of ministries but it is fascinating to see Paul using the words 'first' and 'second' in relation to apostolic and prophetic ministries. As a committed evangelical I would have expected to see the role of teachers listed as of second order priority because of the importance of teaching the Word of God to the Church.

But this is not what Scripture teaches us! Apostolic leadership is always primary for the ministry of the church, (and let's praise the Lord for the way he's restoring this to his church in these times!) but it seems that before the teachers can teach, the Church needs to know from the Lord what he actually wants his people to be taught at a particular time. For this the Church first needs the help of its prophetic ministers.

In the previous chapter I wrote that the Lord, as our good shepherd, loves to lead his Church by his voice. So it is essential that

Church leaders grow in hearing the Lord's voice for themselves, but we cannot expect them to do all of it for the Church. And here Paul reminds us that God actually appoints prophetic ministers to exercise this role of being watchmen (and women) for his Churches. Their primary role and calling is to seek the Lord and to listen to him so that they can assist the Church to hear the Lord's voice behind them saying 'This is the way; walk in it'. (Isa 30:21)

Not long after we had had the benefit of David Parker's teaching amongst us in Harrow, I sensed the Lord urging me to gather around myself a small group of people who were gifted in intercession and prophecy. I sensed Him say to me that they should be people who had a deep love for Him and His Church, a sound grasp of the Bible, and should be people who really prayed for the Church. Over the years this group has been an enormous blessing to me. Time and again the Lord has given me direct guidance, encouragement, warnings and vision through their ministry. No Church leader should be without a group like this!

5. For Prayer

On one occasion Jesus said 'I tell you that if two of you on earth agree about anything you ask for, it will be done for you by my Father in heaven. For where two or three come together in my name, there I am with them'. (Matt 18:19,20) Here he is saying that if we pray in agreement for something which is in accordance with his character and his will then we can be assured that that prayer will be answered.

The value of prophecy is obvious here. If we spend time waiting on the Lord, asking him to show us what *he* wants us to pray about, and we then go on to ask for whatever he has revealed, we are allowing the Holy Spirit to lead our prayer. And as Paul wrote to the Church in Rome, 'faith comes from hearing the message and the message is heard through the word of Christ'. (Rom 10:17) If we are praying for what we believe the Lord has told us to pray for, we will pray with much more faith, because he will surely answer prayers that he has inspired.

Leaders need to be aware that the Church prayer meeting is one of the best places in which the use of the gift of prophecy, and prophetic ministries can be encouraged. Church prayer meetings usually attract people who have a stronger prophetic gifting, because people who hear the Lord are more easily moved by him to pray, and therefore usually find greater fulfilment in prayer.

In prayer meetings, I sometimes like to encourage people to follow these steps:

1. Consciously come into the Lord's presence and worship him.

2. Then sit in silence before him for up to ten minutes, asking him to speak about what he wants us to pray for.

3. Then I ask the first person who feels moved to share what is on their heart to do so, asking others at the meeting to pray about that issue until we sense the Lord telling us to move on.

4. Then I ask the next person who feels the Lord's prompt to share what they have heard to do so, and this is then prayed for, and so on....

In meetings like these there can sometimes be a wonderful sense of the way the Lord is leading the group in prayer. It also brings a deep sense of spiritual agreement in people's hearts as they pray together for what they believe he has spoken. And they also go home feeling refreshed and encouraged because there is a deep sense that if the Lord has led them to pray that way, there is every reason to believe that he will also answer these prayers.

6. Warning, correction and rebuke

The Bible gives many examples of how God can bring warning, rebuke or correction through prophecy. Joseph was warned that Herod intended to kill Jesus through an angel appearing to him in a dream (Matt 2:13). After King David had committed adultery with Bathsheba, the Lord sent the prophet Nathan with a prophetic parable as a rebuke to David for what he had done (2 Sam 12:1-13).

Earlier in this chapter I refer to a prophetic group who have been very helpful to me in my ministry. Some years ago one of them gave me a picture of a car stopped at red traffic lights. But the driver of the car was wanting to cross the lights when they were still red! She then went on to say that she believed that I was the driver of that car, that there were a few others in the car with me, and it seemed that I was wanting to jump the lights. She then referred to a para-church organisation linked to the parish and said that she believed that this picture had something to do with that organisation. She said 'The Lord says "Pray for hidden things to be revealed".'

Now she had no idea that only three days before giving me this prophecy I had been approached by the trustees of a property used by this para-church organisation with the offer to hand over the trusteeship to our Church. This was something the Church had prayed for for many years, and so the offer had seemed like a wonderful answer to prayer to me! I and our Churchwardens were wanting to take over responsibility for the Trust as soon as possible.

However, this prophetic warning led us to be far more careful, and without going into any detail, this saved us from taking on a substantial legal liability for problems we weren't then aware of. We later still took over the trusteeship, but were able to indemnify ourselves from these liabilities. I am still grateful to the Lord for this timely warning!

On another occasion I was helping with a retreat for Church leaders in Finland. At one point I was walking down the corridor of the retreat centre. Ahead of me I saw one of the kitchen staff there speaking to two Finnish members of the retreat. As I looked at him I sensed the Lord say to me 'Warn him that he drives his car too fast!'. When approached them I asked one of the leaders to ask this man in Finnish if he sometimes drove his car too fast. As he heard this he looked at me in a quizzical sort of way, and then said ' Well, I did actually get a speeding fine last week'. I then told him what I believed the Lord had said to me and that I felt that the Lord was warning him that if he didn't slow down he was at risk of having a serious accident.

But as these words were spoken to him he was visibly touched by the Holy Spirit, and words of knowledge about his childhood started coming to me. He had been abandoned by his parents when he was very young and had grown up with many problems in his life. He told us how he had been in juvenile detention, and later in prison in early adult life, and how after this his marriage had broken up. And even as we spoke, the Holy Spirit touched him more and more powerfully, pouring the Lord's love and healing into his heart.

These are just some of the ways I have seen prophecy bring great help and blessing to individual Christians and whole Churches. In writing about them I have separated out these different ways, but often one prophecy will fulfil several of these dimensions at the same time.

Having seen the power prophetic gifts have to help us, I long to see Christians and Churches using prophecy far more commonly and extensively in our common life.

CHAPTER THREE

PROPHECY AND EVANGELISM

What lies at the heart of evangelism?

After his death and resurrection, Jesus told his disciples to wait in Jerusalem for the promised gift of the Holy Spirit. As a result of this, they would receive power to '...be my witnesses, in Jerusalem, and in all Judea and Samaria, and to the ends of the earth.'(Acts 1:8). We are still living in the fulfilment of that promise, wherever we are in the world.

But what does this mean? I think he was telling us all that as a result of our being filled with his Spirit, we would be given supernatural enabling to help others to discover that :

- he is God

- he knows all about them

- he loves them and forgives them all their sins

- it is possible to have a living personal relationship with Him through faith in the Lord Jesus Christ

- he has the power and desire to give them his (eternal) life.

There are not many accounts in the gospels of Jesus doing personal (one to one) evangelism. Two notable stories are Jesus meeting with Zaccheus, the short tax collector in Jericho (Lk 19:1-10) and Jesus meeting with the woman at the well at Sychar in Samaria (Jn 4:1-42). In both these stories Jesus' use of revelation made a profound impact on Zaccheus and the Samaritan woman's hearts.

For Zacchaeus, it was the fact that God told Jesus his name, (God knew all about him, despite Jesus having never met him before), and loved him enough to want his Son to stay at his home (a man who was despised and rejected by those around him in Jericho now offered friendship with God), that led Zaccheus to make such a heartfelt response to Jesus.

At the beginning of his account of Jesus meeting with the Samaritan woman, John tells us that this passage has much to teach us about personal evangelism (see John chapter 4 verse 1 and 35).

When Jesus first saw the Samaritan woman coming to draw water alone at the middle of the day, he would immediately have concluded that she was probably shunned by the other women in Sychar. In those days women usually went out *together* to draw water in the morning. His compassion for her would then have led him to ask the Father why she was rejected by the other women, and it is most likely that it was at *this* point that he received revelation about her (that she had been married to five husbands and was now living with another man), before she ever arrived at the well.

Jesus probably then asked the Father for a word of wisdom as to how to broach this sensitive subject with her! And so he was led to ask *her* to draw water for *him* from the well, and then in response make the offer of living water to her.

Later, at the appropriate moment he used another word of wisdom, inviting her to call her husband and come back to the well. Jesus already knew what her true situation was, but this request allowed her to reply truthfully that she had no husband. This in turn allowed the Lord to lovingly affirm her as a very truthful woman, saying that 'You are right when you say you have no husband. The fact is, that you have had five husbands, and the man you now have is not your husband.' And he then reaffirmed her yet again for her truthfulness, by saying 'What you have just said is quite true'.

When she responded 'Sir, I can see that you are a prophet!' she was in effect saying these things:-

1. I can see that you know God, and enjoy a living personal relationship with him.

2. You can hear what he says to you, even about me!

3. He has shown me, through you that he knows all about me, my circumstances and personal history, and still loves me.

All this had great impact on her! It immediately led her to start asking Jesus questions about how to know God in the only terms that she and other Samaritans understood, (i.e. where it was appropriate to go with others to worship). Jesus then revealed his true identity to her, and shortly afterwards we see her *running* back to Sychar- now already herself an evangelist! - calling to others to 'Come, see a man who told me everything I ever did!'.

What had happened here? Very simply, through that word of revelation, Jesus had shown her that God was real, knew all about her, and was deeply interested in her life. This is an essential first stage in evangelism!

Because I have to fly quite regularly as part of my work, I sometimes pray that the Lord will bring someone to sit next to me who he wants me to talk to about him. Some time ago I prayed for this when boarding a flight from London to Finland that went via Copenhagen. So it was with some interest that I watched to see who would come down the aisle to sit next to me! It turned out to be a smartly dressed woman in her 40s, who sat down and immediately started to read her newspaper, ignoring me completely.

Even after we had climbed to cruising altitude she still continued to show no interest in any conversation with me. So I prayed ' Lord, *how* am I going to open a conversation with her?' I sensed him say to me 'Why don't you ask me for some revelation about her?'

I did so, and some thoughts immediately started coming into my mind. I felt him say that she did not know him, that she was gifted as a teacher, and was someone who had a real concern for issues of justice, and particularly justice for oppressed peoples in the world. I also sensed him say to me that she travelled as part of her work, but

I immediately dismissed this because the fact that she was on an aeroplane with me suggested this anyway.

A little later she put down her newspaper. I seized the opportunity to introduce myself, and told her that I was going to attend a Christian conference in Finland. I asked her if she was travelling home to Scandinavia or whether she lived in London. She replied very briefly that she was flying to join her husband for a weekend in Scandinavia, and that she was living in London.

She then reached for her newspaper, and at that moment I sensed the Lord say to me 'Use what I have given you!' . So with my heart in my mouth (because you always doubt whether you have heard the Lord correctly in these situations!), I said 'You're probably going to think me crazy, but as Christians we believe that it's possible for us to know Jesus in a personal way, and that sometimes he speaks to us, either for ourselves or about other people.'

Even as I was saying this I could see that look in her eyes which suggested 'Oh no, here's another religious nutter!', so I quickly added 'And I believe he's just said some things to me about you.' She stopped picking up her newspaper, and now looked at me with new interest. (I guess at the very least she thought this might be as interesting as reading her horoscope in the newspaper!) I went on to tell her what I felt the Lord had shown me, with real trepidation in my heart because I knew that if I'd got it wrong, we still had to sit together for at least another hour of flying!

But even before I'd finished speaking to her she was looking at me in astonishment. It turned out that she was a lecturer in international law in London, that her subject was law relating to international human rights, (particularly those of oppressed peoples!), and that she frequently had to travel as part of her work.

Her newspaper remained on the floor for the rest of the flight. From that moment on she literally peppered me with questions like - 'How is it possible to hear God say things like that to you?' 'When did you learn to hear things from God?', and 'Can anybody learn to do this?'

For the rest of the flight I was able to tell her how I came to know the Lord, experience his love and learn to hear his voice. It was then easy to talk about the basic truths of the gospel in that context. We were still talking together as we left the aircraft! On the way into the airport building I was able to find out that she lived close to a Church that regularly ran Alpha Courses, so I gave her their telephone number, and suggested that she go along to the next course.

Now I don't know whether she actually did so, but what I do know is that the Lord made himself very real to her that day, showed her that he knew all about her, loved her, and was very interested in her life. I doubt that much else would have opened such a useful conversation on that flight!

This is what ordinary Christians can do! I believe the Lord is longing to give many of us opportunities to speak to people for him by opening doors into their hearts through a word of knowledge, a gift of prophecy, or by touching people with his healing love and power. More than that, he is looking to us to ask him for these opportunities, and then be ready for them when he gives them to us.

Another example comes to mind. Someone who used to worship with us here in Harrow (who I will call Jane - not her real name) was praying at her office desk one morning, committing her day's work to the Lord. As she did so, she sensed the Lord say to her that she should go downstairs to her secretary (not a Christian) and offer to talk with her because she had experienced a very painful row at home the night before.

Still wondering whether this really was the Lord, Jane was obedient to this inner prompting, and went downstairs. She said to her secretary 'You know I'm a Christian. I was praying a moment ago, and felt that God may have told me that rather painful things happened in your home last night' Even as she spoke these words, the secretary started weeping, and it became obvious that the Holy Spirit was now touching her deeply.

So Jane suggested that they go to a room where they could have some privacy. There they talked together, and she later welcomed Jane's offer to pray with her. Even as they prayed, more of the Spirit's love and power came upon her, and she came into a very deep experience of the Lord that day.

There is an old Chinese proverb that says 'If a tree falls in the forest and there isn't anyone there, is there any sound?' The point here is - are we willing to make ourselves available to the Lord to be able to hear what he might want to say to us when we are out among people in our everyday lives? This, I believe is one of the main reasons why John recorded the story about Jesus speaking to the

Samaritan woman at the well. He wanted to show us how these things are possible for us too. And I have now experienced the truth of this many times when I have met complete strangers and through revelation the Lord has given me, have found this opening them up to have excellent discussions about him.

CHAPTER FOUR

THE PROPHETIC PERSON

Prophecy is a powerful spiritual gift because when using it correctly we are speaking for God himself, and those we speak to are invited to receive it that way too. It is therefore a gift which can be very easily abused.

So as we seek to obey the teaching of the Bible that we should not only eagerly desire all the spiritual gifts, but be especially keen to learn to prophesy, there are certain fundamental things that we need to know and understand as we embark on that journey. Here are some important things that will help to keep us from abusing this wonderful gift.

1. Our first ministry is always to the Lord himself.

All Christians are members of Jesus' royal priesthood, and the first ministry of any priest is always first to God. Ultimately it is true to say that if we do not have a ministry to the Lord in worship, prayer and listening to him, we do not have a ministry in his Name to anyone else. And because prophecy is such a powerful gift, it is very easy to fall for the temptation to be more excited about exercising the gift than we are about the Giver himself.

Somewhere around 1990 there was a prophetic word given to the Churches in the UK in which the Lord said to us 'Seek my face, not my hands'. By this he meant that we should be seeking him for his own sake rather than only seek him for the gifts that he gave to help us do exciting ministry.

There is a saying 'Knowledge is power' and it is not uncommon for prophetically gifted people to try to unconsciously (or sometimes even consciously) exploit the revelation that they get to gain influence within their Churches.

The corrective to all of this is to pray for increased desire to meet with the Lord, and to enjoy intimacy with him, and that he leads us to take care to build sound disciplines of prayer into the pattern of our lives. The Bible tells us that there is an intimate connection between reverence for the Lord and our ability to hear his voice. The Psalmist tells us 'The Lord confides *(speaks intimately and privately)* in those who fear him' (Ps 25:14 - my amplification in italics).

2. Know yourself loved by the Lord !

'God is love, whoever lives in love lives in God and God in him.' (1 Jn 4:16) Everything God does or says is an expression of his loving, holy nature. This is why Paul urges us to 'follow the way of love' when we exercise spiritual gifts and particularly the gift of prophecy. 'It is out of the overflow of the heart that the mouth speaks.' (Lk 6:45) In fact love is God's channel through which all his gifts flow.

For this reason it is of first priority that we know the Lord's love for ourselves, and are secure in his favour upon our lives as we seek to grow in using his gifts. Those who are truly secure in his love are far less likely to import their own agendas, 'need to be needed', or other distortions into what they believe the Lord may be saying to them.

So whenever we seek the Lord for a prophetic word for a person or the Church it is very important that we first pray that the Lord will fill our hearts again with his love for us, and give us his love for those to whom we may speak in his name. This helps to ensure that we are doing this ministry with the right motives. *Having any other motive* quickly opens us up to the distortions which emanate from our own spirits, or worse still from the evil one himself.

Let's remember that when Jesus told his disciples that he was going to go up to Jerusalem and be handed over to the authorities, be flogged, condemned and crucified, Peter remonstrated with him and said 'Never Lord. This shall never happen to you!' (Matt 16:22). We then read that Jesus turned and said to Peter 'Get behind me, Satan! You are a stumbling-block to me; you do not have in mind the things of God, but the things of men.' Jesus would never have addressed Peter as Satan. It is quite clear that he had discerned that Satan was actually speaking through Peter at that point. And this had been made possible because Peter was following his own agenda rather than being open to that of the Lord.

3. A heart to know and understand the Bible

The Bible is God's inspired and authoritative Word to us. Through it we come to know and understand more of the Lord's nature, purposes and plans for his world, the truth about the human condition, our need of salvation, and supremely about the Lord Jesus Christ himself.

It is absolutely essential for every aspect of our Christian lives that we have a regular, disciplined pattern of reading the Bible so that we can grow in our knowledge of God. This is especially important if we are going to learn to use the gift of prophecy, because it is as we feed on holy Scripture that we give the Holy Spirit the opportunity to form the mind of Christ within us. (1 Cor 2:16) To put it another way, the word of God in Scripture will 'tune' our spiritual radio receivers within us to be 'on net' with the transmission from heaven.

There is a beautiful promise in Isaiah 54 v13 'All your sons will be taught by the Lord'. When we have come to know the Lord and are filled with his Spirit, he loves to make the Scriptures come alive to us and to teach us to know his ways. This then helps us to recognise his voice when he is speaking to us. So we are being completely unrealistic if we are hungry to grow in using the gift of prophecy, but don't match this with an even more serious commitment to growing in listening to God's Word for ourselves.

4. A heart commitment to growing in Christ-like character

Jesus said 'Blessed are the pure in heart for they shall see (and hear) God' . (Matt5:8 my amplification in brackets). We see this principle beautifully illustrated in Moses life. In the book of Numbers we read of Miriam and Aaron being jealous of Moses' ability to hear from God, and the authority this then gave him among the people (Num 12:1-8a).

The first clue as to why Moses saw and heard the Lord so clearly is seen in verse 3, where we are told 'Now Moses was a very humble man, more humble than anyone else on the face of the earth' . Later in verse 6 we see God saying to Miriam and Aaron 'When a prophet of the Lord is among you, I reveal myself to him in visions, I speak to him in dreams. But this is not true of my servant Moses; he is faithful in all my house. With him I speak face to face, clearly and not in riddles; he sees the form of the Lord. Why then were you not afraid to speak against my servant Moses?'

Here the Lord was saying that because Moses was always obedient to whatever he said to him, he spoke with Moses clearly and not in riddles, even face to face. With other 'prophets' whose hearts were not as pure as Moses' heart was, the Lord chose to speak in riddles, in dreams, visions and unclear things. We need to understand that this is for our protection! The more clearly we hear God speak to us, the more we become accountable to him for our response to what he has said to us.

But it also needs to be stressed that the spiritual gift of prophecy is one of the 'charismata', that is 'workings of God's grace'. God never gives these gifts because we have earned or deserved them through merit of our own. They are always expressions of his loving grace towards us and the people to whom he wants us to speak. This is why somebody who is a very new Christian who has only recently been filled with the Holy Spirit can use the gift of prophecy, even when there is perhaps much in their lives that needs to be put right before God.

It is also true, however, that as we grow into a Christ-like character and in obedience to the Lord, the Lord can then trust us with clearer and stronger revelation because he has already found us faithful in handling lesser revelation in times past.

It is very interesting to note that one of the key Hebrew words in the Old Testament that is translated 'hear' can be equally translated 'obey'. The Bible does not draw a distinction between these two things because we cannot sit in judgment over what God says to us. In fact, to seek the Lord for a prophetic word to be used for our own, rather than his, purposes is the same as the sin of divination. (See 1Sam15:22-23).

It is those who want to grow in their love for the Lord and obedience to his word, whether in Scripture or any direct prophetic word that he might speak, who will hear the Lord better and better. Psalm 32 has a wonderful promise from the Lord. He assures us 'I will instruct you and teach you in the way you should go; I will counsel you and watch over you. Do not be like the horse or the mule, which have no understanding but must be controlled by bit and bridle or they will not come to you.' (Ps 32:8,9)

5. A heart strong in the Lord's grace

As mentioned earlier, the Greek word that Paul uses for 'spiritual gifts' is 'charismata', of which one is the gift of prophecy. Charismata literally means working of God's grace and it is vital that we understand that the Lord gives these beautiful gifts not because we deserve them, but because he loves to give them - through us - to bless others. The only basis on which we can ever expect any gift from the Lord is that of the righteousness of Jesus imputed to us through faith.

So those who want to grow in their effectiveness in exercising spiritual gifts need to grow into solid confidence in their standing before the Lord that he has graciously provided for *them* through the finished work of Christ on the cross. They also need to be consciously aware of his wonderful favour as something fixed upon their lives. This is essential, because anyone who is serious in their desire to use these gifts for God's purposes very soon experiences the reality of spiritual warfare, in which the enemy seeks to quench their faith and confidence in the Lord's grace towards them.

CHAPTER FIVE

SOME BASICS TRUTHS ABOUT PROPHECY

As mentioned earlier, we must always base our expectations of the Lord on what is taught in the Bible. So, if we're to grow in exercising the gift of prophecy, we need to know what the Bible shows about some of the different ways that God speaks to us, and through us to others.

Ways that God speaks shown us in the Bible

1. Particular verses in the Bible 'quickened' to us by the Holy Spirit

Any Christian who has been born of the Spirit will know those times when you are reading the Bible and a certain verse, or passage 'leaps off the page at you'. You have that immediate inner 'knowing' that the Holy Spirit is saying 'I am speaking to you now through this verse about these (present) circumstances in your life.' While you couldn't prove this to another person, you simply 'know' that the Lord is speaking to you in this direct and personal way.

Whenever I particularly need to hear the Lord speak to me about a problem or a decision that I need to make, the first place to which I always go is the Bible. And I now would not be without the Anglican Lectionary! This is a Church of England scheme that appoints Bible readings (a Psalm, an Old Testament and a New Testament reading for Morning and Evening Prayer every day of the year).

I usually read each day from the morning lectionary for my own times of prayer. But if I particularly want to ask the Lord for guidance over some issue, I normally first try to clarify what my question to him is (because usually the clearer your question is, the easier it is to discern his answer!), and then read the three appointed readings. Sometimes I sense nothing clear at all, and conclude that the Lord may not be choosing to speak to me about it in that occasion and need to wait. But often I find that he speaks to me quite vividly about the issue through all three of the readings.

At one point when I was working as a curate in Notting Hill, I and another leader were waiting on the Lord to confirm whether he wanted us to go ahead and ask for our Church Council's go-ahead to plant a new congregation in St. Peters, Notting Hill. St. Peters had not been used for Sunday morning worship for some time. Then my Vicar called for a special meeting of the staff for Morning Prayer there, something we had never done there before.

So I and the other leader took this as a prompt from the Lord to ask him to speak to us on that occasion. We prayed beforehand, asking the Lord to do so through the lectionary readings in that special weekday morning service.

When we met, the psalm seemed to speak encouraging things about God bringing new life, and the Old Testament reading was from Isaiah, also speaking of God bringing new things into existence, and new life for his people. Encouraging as this was, I still didn't feel that the Lord had spoken clearly enough about whether this meant that he wanted the Church plant to be started. 'Lord, please give us something really clear!!', I prayed, wondering how on earth he could do this, because St. Peters Notting Hill is certainly not mentioned anywhere in the Bible!

One of the staff then got up to read the New Testament lesson. To this day I don't know why she did this, but she first picked up a modern version of the Bible, then put it down and picked up a Revised Version which uses more traditional language. It was the story of Peter's confession of Jesus' true identity in response to his question 'Who do men say that I am?'

As I heard her read the words 'Thou art the Christ, the Son of the living God' I sensed the Lord say within me 'Look up!' I looked up, and there above me, inscribed on the arch over the Church apse where we were seated, were those very words. As I continued to look, the reading went on 'And on this rock will I build my Church.' I and the other leader then looked at each other and knew what the other had 'heard'.

Even though we could never 'prove' to anyone reading this that

that is what God said to us at that moment, we both then knew that he had answered our question. And that began the process that has since resulted in a completely new Church being re-established in that building.

I keep a journal of the things I believe the Lord has spoken to me as I read the Bible. I don't write in it every day, but I now have a record of many things written there that have later been fulfilled by the Lord, sometimes years after he first spoke them to me. He truly is a living, speaking Shepherd who loves to speak to us through his amazing book.

2. Thoughts and impressions

When you are out among people you cannot turn to the Bible every five minutes to seek out revelation for particular situations! For that we need to hear the Lord 'on the hoof'. In my case I find that the Lord speaks to me through thoughts or particular impressions that he gives me.

Paul, writing about Christians says 'But we have the mind of Christ.' (1Cor 2:16). In other words, as we yield our lives to him, his Spirit lives in our minds as well as our bodies. So it stands to reason that as we feed our minds on the Bible, he will not only gradually teach us to think as he does, but from time to time *will think his own particular thoughts through us.*

And if we therefore consciously offer our minds to him in a situation where we need to hear him (in order to do his will), it is perfectly reasonable to expect that his Spirit will bring particular thoughts or impressions into our minds.

This has happened to me more times than I can remember. While I can and often do get it wrong, I am regularly astonished at his goodness and faithfulness in giving these thoughts when I ask for them. I have given examples of this (like 'Tell him I like the way he drinks his beer!') in an earlier section of this book.

3. Pictures, visions

Some people are more visually oriented, and so tend to 'see' things in their mind's eye, rather than 'think' them. In my experience women tend to be rather more visually oriented than men, but that is only on balance, rather than a general rule.

Here people simply 'see' something in their mind's eye. It might be a static or moving picture, or like seeing an old black and white photograph. Jesus 'saw' Nathanael sitting under the fig tree before Philip went to call him (Jn 1:48). Loraine Craig and Freda Meadows, prophetic ministers who travel with me, sometimes 'see' people in the Spirit while in prayer before going out on trips. Then when they meet and recognise them, they give them the prophecies that they saw while in prayer before the trip.

Sometimes people see (in their mind's eye, rather than literally) something appear on the person that they are looking at. John Wimber used to tell the story of how he once looked at a fellow passenger on a flight across America, and saw the word 'adultery' across his forehead. A woman's name then came into his mind, and sensing the prompting of the Lord, he leant across and asked him 'Does the name .... mean anything to you?' The man went pale, and immediately suggested to John that they go to the aircraft's upstairs lounge to talk. This led to a very fruitful evangelistic conversation!

4. Dreams

The Bible has many stories of how God spoke to people through dreams. Joseph was helped to accept Mary's pregnancy, and warned to flee to Egypt with Mary and the infant Jesus through dreams. (Matt 1:20,21, 2:19,20) Paul changed the entire course of a missionary journey and went to Macedonia in response to a vision in a dream of a man from Macedonia saying 'Come over to Macedonia and help us!' (Acts 16:9)

Freda Meadows, mentioned earlier, once gave me very extraordinary confirmation that a Church plant should be closed, and its congregation be amalgamated with another parish Church congregation in our Team Ministry through a dream God gave her. She had had this dream some months before, but did not know what it meant. She was not then at all aware of what I and the other leaders had been discussing.

Only later, as I consulted her about it, she found the Holy Spirit immediately reminding her of the dream, and this gave us both very helpful confirmation of a decision that was going to require very delicate implementation!

5. Through things spoken by others

In the book of Judges there is a wonderful story of how Gideon and his servant Purah overheard a Midianite soldier telling another about a dream he had had. As the other gave the interpretation, Gideon 'knew' that the Lord was speaking to him through what was being spoken. (Judges 7:13-15)

While based in the UK, David Parker told the story of how God spoke to him through a routine tannoy message on the London Underground! At some stations where the railway is on a bend, a prerecorded voice repeats 'Mind the gap!' again and again as passengers alight and board the train.

As David stepped out he heard this, and sensed the Holy Spirit say something like 'Did you hear that David?' So he found a quiet corner and asked the Lord to explain what he meant by this, and heard the Lord tell him to call the Churches to mind the very large gap that had opened up between the culture of the Church and that of the world around us. He later went on to preach this message all around the UK.

Before meetings at which a very important decision needs to be made, I like to ask the Lord to speak his mind about it through someone present (who may have no direct awareness that he is speaking through them in this way!). I vividly remember an occasion where our Church Council faced a very important decision about changes to the structure and timing of our Sunday services.

Because I already had very clear views about which way I felt the decision should go, I and a Churchwarden prayed beforehand that the Lord would express his mind through someone at the meeting. After much of the discussion had already happened, someone started speaking. He would never have described himself as a charismatic Christian, let alone believe that he exercised the gift of prophecy! But as he spoke quietly and carefully, I sensed a sudden increase of the Lord's presence in the room, and there was a new stillness as he spoke. I and the Churchwarden glanced at one another, and even at that moment we knew that the Lord was answering our prayer. The meeting soon came to sincere agreement to take that bold decision soon after that!

6. Through our circumstances

Often God allows us to go through difficult times, or face apparently impossible obstacles to progress, for the very purpose of getting us to come to him to ask 'What are you saying to us in this situation, Lord?'

In the Bible he assures us that nothing is too difficult for him (e.g. Lk 1:37), and any door he opens cannot be shut, and doors that he closes cannot be opened. (Rev 3:7) In other words, he will always provide us with his way through a task or project that he has already said he wants accomplished. So when there are difficulties or obstacles, this is usually an invitation from him to ask for his guidance or correction about the way we have been going. Often the Holy Spirit will then help us first to see what he is saying through the circumstances themselves, before he gives more revelation about the way forward.

7. Through outward visible things

In the book of Jeremiah we read of God asking Jeremiah 'What do you see, Jeremiah?' His reply was 'I see the branch of an almond tree.' The Hebrew word 'almond' could also mean 'watching', and God then spoke to him through this double meaning about how he (God) was 'watching' to see his word fulfilled in those days. I think it is likely that there was actually an almond tree branch visible to Jeremiah outside his window when that question came to him.

Then God went on to speak even more to him through a tilting pot, which again Jeremiah may have been looking at as God's question came to him. (Jer 1:7-19) Later we see God speaking to Jeremiah through the pot he saw being refashioned on a potter's wheel. (Jer 18:1-6)

God spoke to the prophet Amos through a basket of ripe fruit. We are first told that God pointed out this basket, and asked Amos what he saw, before then speaking to him about the time being ripe for him to bring judgment upon his people. (Am 7:1-2)

Some years ago I was driving through countryside on my way to speak at a leaders' retreat. It was late November, getting dark, and the leaves had fallen off the trees for the winter. As I drove, I suddenly saw a tree rather like a cherry tree in full blossom! I then immediately sensed the Lord say to me 'Did you see that tree, Bruce?' I replied 'Yes, Lord. Are you saying something to me through this?' I believe his reply was - 'Tell my people that I am bringing springtime to my Church, while at the same time I am bringing winter to the world. This will help more and more people to see where they can come to the true source of my life again.'

In other words the Church is going to experience more and more renewal, while in the world around us, things are going to go from bad to worse. I believe this word is being fulfilled in these times, and that the pace of both processes will steadily accelerate in the years ahead.

Often when we offer personal prophetic ministry, we find the Lord drawing our attention to things that we see. He may draw our attention to the shape of someone's shoes, the kind of earrings a lady wears, or some other feature of their body or attire.

There are obvious dangers of turning this into a method in place of listening directly to the Lord, but I find that where it happens, I first sense the Lord drawing my attention to something so that I then question him about it. After listening to the Lord this way I then close my eyes and ask him to speak to me through an inward picture or thought.

8. Through an audible voice

I cannot ever recall hearing the Lord speak to me audibly, but I know some people for whom this happens from time to time. This was how God spoke for the first time to Samuel when as a boy his mother had left him with the priest Eli in the Temple in Jerusalem. God's voice was so clearly audible that Samuel was convinced that it was Eli calling to him three times! Only after the third time did Eli himself realise that Samuel was hearing the voice of the Lord in this audible way, and told him how to wait on the Lord and hear his voice. (1 Sam 3)

I suspect that God usually only speaks this clearly to people who have a calling to a more significant prophetic ministry, but we need to see that God does sometime choose to speak like this.

9. Through a supernatural gift of interpretation of a prophetic tongue

Paul taught the Corinthian Churches that while the most common purpose of the spiritual gift of tongues (other languages) was to enable believers to express worship to God in a language of heaven given by the Holy Spirit which we would not usually understand. (1Cor 14:2)

But sometimes in a Christian meeting the Holy Spirit may inspire a 'prophetic' tongue, where the tongue is addressed to the congregation rather than to God. In this case the congregation must wait (and pray!) that the Holy Spirit will give the gift of an interpretation of this (unintelligible) tongue to someone in the congregation so that everyone may grasp its meaning, and therefore what the Lord is saying to them. (1Cor 14:13)

Incidentally, I am personally convinced that it is this use of speaking in tongues that Paul discourages where it is ever done without being followed by proper interpretation. It would seem that immature Corinthian Christians were parading their 'super-spirituality' by giving solo demonstrations of their ability to use the gift of tongues, and Paul wrote to stop this practice.

But some Christians today press this teaching to mean that Christians should therefore never use this gift corporately as part of spoken or sung worship, or on occasions in simultaneous corporate intercession. I believe this is to press Paul's teaching too far. While not clear enough to be used as a proof text, Paul does seem to commend the use of singing in tongues ('singing in the Spirit') in his letter to the Ephesian Church, where he suggests that we should use a mix of psalms, hymns and spiritual songs in our worship. And his exhortation that Christians should not be drunk with wine (leading to singing in a debauched state??) but rather that we should go on and on being filled with the Holy Spirit immediately precedes this teaching about Spirit-filled singing. (Eph 5:18,19)

If a Church has had mature teaching about the nature and practical use of the gifts of the Holy Spirit, and the possibility of corporate singing in tongues is explained by the worship leader, I see no reason why this practice should not be actively encouraged. Many times I have seen the Holy Spirit come very powerfully upon gatherings where he has been allowed to inspire sung or spoken worship in this way!

Know that there are different dimensions of prophecy

It is very important that we realise that there are three basic dimensions of prophecy. These are:

The revelation given to someone.

This is what they heard, thought, saw, dreamt etc from God, and it is very important that they and we take note of this at *face value*.

The interpretation of this revelation.

This refers to the *meaning* of the revelation that was received. While the interpretation may be immediately clear to the person who received the initial revelation, this is not always the case. It is sometimes very easy to read our own interpretations into a genuine revelation, or it may be that sometimes the Lord wants to give the interpretation through another or others as they pray about the original revelation.

Those who are in Church leadership need to be especially careful in this regard when handling prophecies that are brought to them, or spoken in meetings. We can very easily dismiss a whole prophecy because we have rightly rejected its *interpretation*, and leave the person giving the prophecy feeling very hurt and confused. This is because they may well have received genuine *revelation* but confused it with wrong *interpretation*.

When people bring me prophecies, I usually ask them to write them down, separating, if possible, the original revelation from what they felt it meant to them. If we later find a truer interpretation, it allows us to go back to them to *affirm* their gifting, but giving them help in learning how to interpret prophecy.

This way of doing things avoids the frequent sense of rejection that can come to people who may be fairly new to prophecy, and brings both encouragement and instruction.

The application of the prophecy.

This refers questions like 'Who is this prophecy for?' or 'When will it come about?' This is the area in which Christians are most frequently (and sometimes notoriously!) wrong when handling prophecy, and we should be very careful to avoid being too adamant that we are right in these respects.

For example, there were some very specific prophecies given in the mid 1990's that revival was going to break out in England in a specific year that has now passed. That was not fulfilled, but I believe these people *did* hear that the Lord is preparing both his Church and the nation for a very major time of revival. It was just the timing (application) of these prophecies that obviously been wrong.

Sometimes the Lord wants to give more detail of the application of a prophecy to a group of people bearing leadership responsibility in a Church, or across Churches in a city or a nation, rather than give all of this when the prophecy is first received by someone. In this way he draws the attention of others to the thrust of what the prophecy is saying, and forms the team of leaders that he needs for its outworking. Those who know the story of what has happened in recent years among the Churches in Cali, Columbia, will know that this is how God's work developed there.

Know that prophecy is available to the church today

It is likely that you are reading this book because you already believe that the gift of prophecy is available to the Church today. Sadly there are not a few evangelical and other Christians who are far from convinced of this! I know I am touching on a big subject here, but I would like to show some clear Bible evidence for why I firmly believe that this gift is freely available for us today.

In between his teaching on the gifts and ministries of the Holy Spirit in his first letter to the Corinthians chapters 12 and 14, we read Paul's magnificent chapter on love, showing how it is love that should always be both the motivation and manner for the use of the gifts of the Spirit.

In it he says 'Love never fails. But where there are prophecies, they will cease; where there are tongues, they will be stilled; where there is knowledge, it will pass away'. (1Cor 13:8) So Paul says there definitely *will* be a time when prophecy and the other gifts of the Spirit will come to an end and no longer be needed. The vital question to ask here of this text is *when* this time will come.

That is what Paul immediately goes on to answer. 'For we know in part and we prophesy in part, but when perfection comes, the imperfect disappears.' (1Cor 13:9,10) This is Paul's first hint of *when* we will no longer need the gifts of the Holy Spirit. He then goes on to say 'When I was a child, I talked like a child, I thought like a child, I reasoned like a child. When I became a man, I put childish ways behind me.' (1Cor 13:11) Some evangelical Christians claim that the perfection that Paul speaks of here is the closure of the canon of holy Scripture, when the Church decided once and for all on what writings constituted the contents of the Bible.

But this surely cannot be what Paul is saying here. He goes on to write 'Now we see but a poor reflection as in a mirror, then we shall see face to face. Now I know in part; then I shall know fully, even as I am fully known.' (1 Cor 13:12) There is only one time when we shall see the Lord face to face or know him fully even as he already fully knows us. That will be *when he returns at his second coming*. And as the first verse of the following chapter makes plain, Paul wants us to follow the way of love and eagerly desire all the gifts of the Holy Spirit, especially the gift of prophecy, until the Lord returns.

I have to add that I have seen too many people blessed *in biblical ways* through the exercise of different gifts of the Holy Spirit to now even begin to doubt that this is the truth of what the Bible shows us. And in this first letter to the Corinthians, a Church that had been *abusing* the gifts of the Holy Spirit, Paul is plainly urging them to seek and *use* these gifts, but to do so in a mature and loving way.

CHAPTER SIX

KNOW THAT YOU CAN DO IT !

Truths that help us to grow in using our prophetic gifting

As mentioned in the last chapter, the first key step in growing in supernatural things is to know the truth about them. So what else do we need to know about prophecy in order to start actually using this gift?

Know that all *Christians can exercise the gift of prophecy*

In his first letter to the Corinthians Paul makes it quite clear that only some within the body of Christ are called to exercise a prophetic *ministry* (see his list of different ministries in 1 Cor 12:27-30 and Eph 4:11-13). 1 Corinthians 14, however, seems to make it clear that Paul expected that all Christians could use the *gift* of prophecy from time to time.

In Ch14 v 1 he urges all of them to desire the gifts of the Spirit and especially the gift of prophecy. Now here he could be referring to a *corporate* desire to see these things exercised. In verse 5, however, he says 'I would like every one of you to speak in tongues, but I would rather have you *(every one of you!)* prophesy' (my amplification in italics). Again it could be argued that here we are simply seeing Paul's enthusiasm for the exercise of this gift in the Church! But later in this chapter Paul writes 'For you can *all* prophesy in turn so that *everyone* may be instructed and encouraged.' (1Cor 14:31)

Some teachers argue against this view, saying that only some Christians are designated by the Holy Spirit to use one or other of His gifts. They base this on 1 Cor 12: 7-11 where Paul writes 'To one there is given through the Spirit the message of wisdom, to another the message of knowledge by means of the same Spirit,.. to another prophecy,' (1 Cor 12: 8-10).

But this is to completely misinterpret what Paul is saying here. The context of this passage is the *Church* when it is gathered together, and Paul is here emphasising that at any *particular* meeting the Holy Spirit will be in control of who he uses to express one or other of his gifts. So on one occasion a particular person might be used to utter a gift of prophecy, but on another occasion that same person might be used to speak out a word of knowledge. The clear focus in this section is the Lordship of the Holy Spirit over the meeting, distributing his gifts as he pleases. (1 Cor 12: 11)

In the early days of charismatic renewal, this wrong view of how the gifts of the Spirit are distributed among Christians led many to ask the question 'What is my gift?'. This is not the right question!

As Paul goes on to show in the next section of chapter 12, the correct question to ask is 'What is my role or *ministry* within the body of Christ?', 'Am I a hand, an eye or foot within the body of Christ?'

Thus those with a prophetic ministry will have the calling to be the eyes or ears of the body of Christ and they will therefore be given a stronger prophetic gifting than is typical of other members of the Church.

For most *ministries* within the Church we will need to use a cluster of the gifts of the Holy Spirit. For example, those who offer personal prayer ministry after a service as members of the Church ministry team, may need to use a word of knowledge to discern what the Lord wants to do for somebody, a word of wisdom to follow the Lord's guidance as to how to minister to that person, and the spiritual gift of faith through which a gift of healing may then be released. They might also then be given a word of prophecy for that person to strengthen them for their onward walk with the Lord! If everyone was allowed to operate in only just one spiritual gift by the Holy Spirit we would need enormous ministry teams, with several needing to minister to someone needing prayer!

But someone called to exercise an administrative role within the Church may need to have a visionary gifting to see new possibilities of how God wants things organised, the gift of wisdom to know how those future things might be practically organised in the Church, and even a prophetic gifting to discern which people are appropriate to bear responsibility for different tasks as this work is carried out.

But my main reason for believing that all Christians who are filled with the Holy Spirit can exercise the gift of prophecy is set out in the section below.

Know what it means to be born again!

We turn now to the familiar story of the night-time visit of Nicodemus to talk to Jesus. (John Chapter 3).

Nicodemus was attracted to Jesus because it was quite clear to him that God was expressing himself in many supernatural ways through Jesus. 'Rabbi, we know you are a teacher who has come from God. For no-one could perform the miraculous signs you are doing if God were not with him.' (Jn 3:2) This statement implies a question. The question is 'It is clear that God is doing supernatural things through you, but *how* does this happen? How do you do these things with God?'

Now Nicodemus was plainly not aware that he was speaking to the second Person of the Holy Trinity, now incarnate in the world. But as I have tried to show earlier in this book, God's Son voluntarily laid aside his divine glory when he came to live amongst us, and being found in human form chose, for our sake, to do his supernatural ministry *in his humanity* through the anointing and gifting of the Holy Spirit.

It is to this implied question of Nicodemus that Jesus replied, explaining to him how *he (Nicodemus) could also come to see what the Father was doing and hear what he was saying.* Jesus told him 'I tell you the truth, no-one can see the Kingdom of God unless he is born again.' (Jn 3: 3) We need to note here that while everything that Jesus said was truth, he sometimes emphasised certain truths as of cardinal importance to Christian life and ministry by adding the words 'I tell you the truth' or 'Truly, truly I say to you ...'

This truth is of key importance to our understanding of renewed ministry, or 'the ministry of the Spirit' as Paul describes it in 2Cor 3:7-18. (i.e. The ministry that has been made possible for Christians through the Cross and since the first outpouring of the Spirit on the day of Pentecost).

We could also turn what Jesus said to Nicodemus the other way round, and this would be equally true. 'Truly, truly I say to you, if someone is born again, they can see the Kingdom of God.' So it is our spiritual birthright, if we are born again, to be able to see what the Father is doing, or to hear his voice so that we can participate in the activities of his Kingdom.

Let us examine more closely what Jesus is saying here. Please think of yourself when you were a small baby within your mother, perhaps only minutes before she first began to be in labour. Compare yourself at that moment with how things were five minutes after the birth process was completed.

If we ask the question 'Did you change as a consequence of that birth process?' the answer is plainly 'No!'. You didn't suddenly grow a tenth toe, or your second ear during the birth process itself. Even your weight probably did not change during that time. In order to understand what Jesus was really saying to Nicodemus we need to ask another question, i.e. 'What difference did the event of birth make for you?' I think the answers below better help us to see what Jesus was saying to Nicodemus.

Awareness of relationship. When you were inside your mother you were truly your mother and father's child. But you were quite incapable of appreciating this fact, and were living within your mother as the centre of your own universe. It was only after you were born, by a power not of yourself, and also not of your own choosing, that you were brought into a position to discover relationship with your mother, and later with other people like your father and siblings.

You then gradually came to know yourself in these relationship to them and later other people too. The same is true spiritually. Before we are born again we do not know God in any personal way, and we live with ourselves as the centre of our universe. Once we are born of the Spirit, (by a power of the Spirit, not of ourselves), we come to know the Lord as our Creator, Saviour and the Lord of our lives. We then learn to give him his rightful place as the Centre of our universe.

Intimacy. Assuming nothing went wrong in the birth process, your mother would almost instinctively have wanted to pick you up and hold you to herself once you were born. This first experience of intimacy was her gift to you. Here again the same is true when we are born again spiritually. I will never forget the sweetness and joy of my first experience of intimacy with the Lord when I came to know Him at the age of 21! When we are born again it is our birthright to know and enjoy intimacy with the Lord, and just as a baby knows when their mother is absent from it, so to we become aware of times when the Lord seems either far away or close to us.

Sight. When you were still inside your mother you only could see lots of her all around you! And when she stood in a well lit room, all was brighter around you. When she got into bed and turned out the lights, all went dark. You would have been aware of this, but nevertheless had no means of *interpreting the meaning or significance of these changes for yourself.* It was only after you were born that you were then able to see the world around you, and gradually learn to interpret the meaning and significance of what you saw.

As Jesus told Nicodemus, this is also true in the realm of the spirit. After the Holy Spirit has brought us to spiritual birth, we can grow in seeing the things of the Kingdom of God, and what God is doing in and around our lives and circumstances through the eye of faith. We now 'live by faith, not by sight.' (2Cor 5:7)

The clearest proof someone has truly been born again is that they have 'seen' who Jesus really is. On one occasion, after Simon Peter had declared 'You are the Christ, the Son of the living God', Jesus said to him 'Blessed are you, Simon, son of Jonah, for this was not revealed to you by man, but by my Father in heaven.' (Matt 16:16,17) If you have 'seen' and truly believe that Jesus is the Christ, the Son of the living God, you too have already been born again.

Hearing. When you were inside your mother you were able to hear sounds. You were probably soothed by the sound of her heartbeat or even the sound of her singing to you! However, for as long as you were within her, you were completely incapable of learning to discern the meaning or significance for your life of the sounds that you were hearing. But after the event of birth, you were suddenly able to hear much more clearly than you could before. From then on you began the slow journey of learning to discern the meaning of the sounds around you, understand language and learn to speak it too.

In fact your parents went to great lengths to help you in this process. I married later in life, and so many of my closest friends married and had children before me. I really struggled when I saw good sensible men I knew well now bending over their new baby, cooing in awful 'baby-talk' to them. They even seemed glad to copy the unintelligible sounds their babies were making to them!

Then I married and later our Tom arrived. Not only did I find myself doing exactly the same things as these friends of mine had done, but I also came to understand why we do this. We even repeatedly copy the sounds our children make to us to establish the very idea of language within them.

Once this is established we start introducing actual words to them, (usually nouns first) by pointing at an object with a simple one-syllable name and repeating its name in a very pointed way. Then one day our child might point to that same object and speak its name. All heaven erupts with joy at that moment! In fact we may even take out the special baby book and write that word in it under the heading 'Baby's first word.'

Why do we do these things? It is simply because we love our children, and know that the cultivation of language is essential if they are to grow into living, personal relationship with us and others around them. And if this is true of us as parents, how much more is this true of our heavenly Father?

Jesus was here telling Nicodemus that it is exactly the same in the realm of the spirit. Once we are born again, we have a clear sense of the reality of God speaking to us personally. It is how we come to realise that we are born again! It was only after we were brought to spiritual birth by the power of the Holy Spirit (through what theologians call the 'prevenient grace' of God) that we were then even in a position to be able to hear the Lord calling to us. (This is clearly shown in verses like 'He who has ears, let him hear.' (Matt 11:15), 'Here I am! I stand at the door *(of your life)* and knock. If anyone hears my voice and opens the door ...' (Rev 3:20 - amplification in italics mine), 'Faith comes by hearing the message and the message is heard through the word of Christ (Rom 10:17)).

And he continues to lead us by his voice, (i.e. the dynamic, living sense of hearing him speak to us). '... and his sheep follow him because they know his voice.' (Jn10:4) Every day of our lives we have the opportunity to grow in recognising and hearing the Lord speak to us. And as I have explained earlier, prophecy is simply learning to use this God-given ability to hear his voice not only for ourselves, but for the benefit of others.

Putting all this together

Do you see what Jesus was explaining to Nicodemus? When Nicodemus was in effect asking Jesus how it was that he was able to see what the Father was doing and hear his voice (because Jesus used to say 'I only do what I see the Father doing' and '... I do nothing on my own, but speak just what the Father has taught me.' (Jn 5:19 and 8:28)) Jesus responded by telling Nicodemus how he too could enter the Kingdom of God and participate in its activities just as Jesus also did.

(However, Jesus never needed to be 'born again'. In his humanity, from conception, he was himself the first of the 'new creation' (2Cor 5:17) Incidentally, this is one key reason why the doctrine of his virgin birth (conception) is so important!)

All this is amazing, wonderful truth! It means that if we are born again of water (by being made one with Jesus through baptism) and the Holy Spirit (the breath of God, who empowers us to live a supernatural, holy life after the pattern of Jesus himself), we too can be led by the Spirit as Jesus was, (e.g. Lk 4:1), and do the things that Jesus did.

The gifts of the Holy Spirit were the spiritual tools Jesus relied on to do his ministry. So if we are born again and are eager in our desire to learn how to operate on the gifts of the Spirit, this is how we too can do what Jesus did.

This is why Jesus could say 'I tell you the truth, anyone who has faith in me will do what I have been doing.' (Jn14:12) And the immediate context of this verse makes it clear that Jesus was speaking of his supernatural miracles.

Once a Christian truly understands these things their life and ministry will never be the same again! Because we have the Giver of God's gifts living within us, and are in a situation that calls for knowledge, wisdom, special faith, spiritual discernment or a word of prophecy from God to help someone, the Giver is there to provide what we need.

And this, too, shows us why it is possible for any Christian born of the Spirit to hear the Lord, both for themselves, and for the benefit of others.

CHAPTER SEVEN

FOLLOWING THE WAY OF WISDOM AND LOVE

Because prophecy is a powerful gift we have to handle it very carefully. We can very easily do real harm if we have either got incorrect revelation for somebody, or have given them correct revelation but in an inappropriate way. Here are some important guidelines for the way we exercise this gift.

1. Our motivation

In 1 Corinthians 14:1 Paul urges the Corinthian Christians to *'Follow the way of love'* and eagerly desire the gifts of the Spirit, especially prophecy. If we seek to exercise the gift of prophecy with anything in our hearts other than love for the Lord and the person or people we may be speaking to, it is all too easy for things to go wrong. For this reason I always urge people to ask the Lord to first fill their hearts with love for those for whom they are praying before they ask him for prophetic gifts for them.

2. *Our purpose*

In the same chapter Paul teaches that prophecies are given within the Church to comfort, strengthen and encourage other Christians.

Sadly some Christians who are genuinely gifted in the prophetic suffer from low self-esteem (often because they can speak out in rather strong black and white terms to others!) and it is all too easy for them to try to elevate themselves by putting others down with a rather critical 'word from the Lord'. They will usually not be aware that this is what they are in effect doing.

All too often 'prophecies' like these run like this: 'Unless the Church repents of (this or that) I, the Lord, will not bless...'. The Bible shows that God does sometimes speak like this to his people, but it is my belief that if he does want to bring a word of correction or discipline to the Church, he will it do through more mature people with a tested prophetic ministry.

For these reasons I would urge anyone wanting to grow in the gift of prophecy to be hungry for words which will strengthen, comfort and encourage as their first priority.

3. *Our manner of giving prophecies*

As Paul also makes clear, all prophecy *must* be weighed and tested. This means that any prophecy could possibly be wrong. We must therefore utter prophecies in a way that reflects this awareness and be gentle and humble in our manner of delivering them.

In some Church circles there has been teaching that suggests that if you sincerely believe that you have received a word from the Lord, you need to speak it out with that sense of authority in your manner of speaking, but we really don't need to do this. 'Following the way of love' means that we should always speak in a manner that leaves our hearers free to weigh what we have said.

So there is no need to preface what we say with the words 'Thus saith the Lord ...'! I think it perfectly in order to preface what we say with words such as 'I think the Lord may be saying something like this ...' because I find that if we are speaking for the Lord with accurate prophecy, the Holy Spirit himself really touches the person or people for whom the word is intended, and bears witness within their own spirit(s) that it is he who is speaking to them. And if a prophecy is not right, that gentle manner of delivering it avoids causing all manner of difficulties for those who hear it.

Paul also taught 'Let your gentleness be evident to all' (Php 4:5). This should be especially the case when we use a gift as potentially powerful as prophecy.

4. Our posture before others

It is also vital that anyone exercising the gift of prophecy does so with a submissive heart. Because prophecy must be weighed, we must be willing to submit what we have spoken or shared to others around us, and especially to our leaders. Beware those within any fellowship who are unwilling to either have their words weighed, or who become strident or difficult when what they have spoken is not accepted by the Church leadership.

This, however, does beg the question 'What do I do if I sincerely believe that I have heard the Lord correctly, but it is not received by others?' This situation may sometimes arise when (for whatever reason) the Church leadership may not be listening properly to the Lord at a given time. But in these circumstances I would urge you to take the matter privately to the Lord in prayer, praying first that he will bless your leaders, and show them by whatever means he chooses that this was truly a word from him. Doing it this way 'preserves the unity of the Spirit in the bond of peace', and the Lord is more than capable of shaking up leaders who are not willing to listen to him.

5. Being wise!

If you ever receive a word of discipline or rebuke for another person, I would urge you to take it someone in pastoral oversight over that person rather than give it directly and immediately to them. First this is because we could have heard wrongly, and the leader can save us from making a dreadful mistake.

If, however, it is correct, we may still need their pastoral wisdom as to how the situation should be handled. Taking this kind of step is an excellent safeguard against bringing the prophetic into disrepute in a Church congregation.

6. Timing

It is important to realise that prophetic words *don't* have to be given immediately after we have received them. Sometimes God gives us prophetic revelation to inform our own prayer for another person and he may never want us to divulge that revelation at all!

For example, if we are praying for a couple who are longing to have a baby and we sense the Lord saying that he is going to give them a child, it would be far better that we simply claim that prophetic word privately in prayer than speak it to them, thereby raising hopes which might be dashed if we were wrong in what we felt we heard.

Sometimes the Lord gives us prophecies which he wants us to hold for a period of time until his Spirit prompts us to speak the word. This is one of the hallmarks of a person who is mature in prophetic gifting. They will sometimes wait for permission to speak a word for some period of time before they actually give it.

Occasionally when praying for another person you may be shown an area of sin in their life, as well as revelation for their strengthening and encouragement. This does not mean that you have to speak all of this to the person! Speak the words of strengthening and encouragement first, and then ask the Lord whether he wants you to share the sensitive issue as well. If you feel you should, it is better to put it in the positive - 'I think the Lord may be wanting to help you in the way that you deal with this or that kind of issue...' rather than say 'I believe the Lord is showing me something sinful in your life'.

As always, the issue here is 'What is the most loving and sensitive way that I can handle this?'

7. Having your ears open to heaven, but your feet on the ground

In his letter to the Romans, Paul urges Christians to prophesy according to the measure of their faith. (see Rom 12: 6b) This statement carries a double meaning, both positive and cautionary.

On the one hand Paul is saying that if you believe that the gift of prophecy is available to be used, then seek to use it! Please note that this verse is set in the context of Paul urging Christians to use the gift or gifts that God has given them, and so it really is an exhortation to step out in this lovely gift.

But, if we are just beginning to use the gift of prophecy, we do need to curtail our expectations of what matters the Lord may choose to speak about to us. This means, for example, that when we are first beginning to use the gift of prophecy we should not expect the Lord to be giving us words for our whole denomination, or words to be sent to the Prime Minister of another nation!

As already mentioned above, I urge those learning to use this gift to get really good at strengthening, comforting and encouraging others in the Church around them before they seek to grow in more weighty use of the gift of prophecy. But this verse from Romans is also a pointer to the way we can grow in our prophetic gifting. Jesus taught that the servant who is faithful with a few things will be given responsibility for more. (Matt 25:23) The more we seek to be used by the Lord in using this and his other gifts, the more he will give us increase in faith to use them.

8. Confusing our emotions with the Spirit

Take great care if you have any personal, emotional involvement in either the subject matter you are prophesying about, or with the person to whom you are giving it! This usually distorts our hearing of the Lord because the place within us that hears the voice of the Lord seems to lie very close to that of our emotions.

Most of us will be familiar with stories of people giving 'prophetic words' that someone is going to be healed of their cancer, when they have later died, or prophecies of marriage for a single person that have not proved true over many years, - or other words in similar vein. When we really love somebody who is in real need, it is especially easy for us to confuse the voice of our emotions and longings with the voice of the Lord.

In conclusion

Be careful in using this gift! It is largely because guidelines like these have been ignored at different times in the Church's history that prophecy has come to be so neglected. Be wise, very loving, and gentle.

CHAPTER EIGHT

STEPPING OUT TO DO IT!

SPIRITUAL PRINCIPLES FOR STEPPING OUT IN PROPHECY

Four key spiritual principles for stepping out in prophecy

We now need to look at some of the spiritual principles involved in learning to do a supernatural thing with God like prophesy. To do this, I want to look at what Paul teaches in his letter to the Church in Rome about growth in something equally supernatural, personal holiness. In chapters 6-8 of this amazing letter, Paul gives very practical teaching of how we can find God's supernatural help to overcome temptation and live out the will of God in our lives.

Space here does not permit a full treatment of this teaching, but Watchman Nee in his remarkable book *The Normal Christian Life* shows that Paul teaches that there are four simple spiritual principles entailed in learning to do supernatural things with God. They can be summarised under the heading of four key words that Paul uses.

Step 1 - Know

This is the first key word and we see Paul using it in verses 3, 6 and 9 of Romans chapter 6 as he begins his teaching on growth in holiness. For Paul, knowledge of the truth about God and what he has done for us in Christ through his death, burial and resurrection is central to our understanding of how we too can be raised to new life in Christ.

This principle holds true for growth in all spiritual things. In John's gospel we read of Jesus saying 'If you hold to my teaching, you are really my disciples. Then you will know the truth, and the truth will set you free' (Jn 8:31,32). This is why it is so important that we have a sound knowledge and grasp of Bible truth, especially when we seek to step out in faith to do supernatural things.

In the case of prophecy we need to know what the Bible teaches about it, the purposes for which God gives it, how it should be weighed and put into practice in the life of the Church. That is the primary aim of what most of this book covers!

Step 2 - Count

Knowledge and understanding are vital and primary, but in themselves they are not enough. There are far too many Christians around who have had much Bible teaching on the gifts of the Holy Spirit, but who are not putting this teaching into practice. (I once heard John Wimber say that the Church was one of the few human institutions that he was aware of that invested so much time and energy in teaching, but so seldom, if ever, gave its people an examination to see whether they were actually *doing* what they had been taught!)

The second key word Paul uses in relation to growth in holiness we see in verse 11 of Romans 6 where he writes 'In the same way, count yourselves dead to sin but alive to God in Christ Jesus'. The Greek word the NIV renders 'count' can also be translated 'reckon', 'deem' or 'consider'. This is more than mere head knowledge. It is a heart conviction that that which you know *about* is actually possible by God's grace for *yourself* personally, not only for Christians generally. This is a realisation that is given to our hearts by the Holy Spirit - 'Wow! God really wants to do this through *me* !'.

This is one important reason why preachers and teachers in renewal will so often ask people to stand or come forward after they have been speaking. At the outset they will pray that the Holy Spirit will bring understanding of the truth to their hearers' minds. But at the end of their teaching it is sometimes very important to invite the Holy Spirit to reveal those truths in a personal way to the hearts of those listening, so that they receive faith to try out what they have just heard about. This faith rises in our hearts as we 'hear' the Holy Spirit speaking to us through the teaching, and touching us in the ministry that follows. ('Faith comes from hearing the message, and the message is heard through the word of Christ.' Rom 10:17)

Step 3 - Offer

But it is not enough to *know* the truth about supernatural things, or even to *count* it possible that you can do these things. Paul says we need to go further than this!

There have been many Christians and indeed Church leaders in the charismatic movement who will say something like this - 'I believe the gifts of the Holy Spirit are available for the Church today, and I am open to the Lord using me or members of my Church in these ways. So if one day he wants to do it, I'm open to it!' Paul is emphatic that we need to go further than this. In regard to growing in holiness he says, 'Do not offer the parts of your body to sin, as instruments of wickedness, but rather offer yourselves to God, as those who have been brought from death to life; and offer the parts of your body to him as instruments of righteousness.' (Rom 6:13)

In other words Paul is saying that we must take an *active step of faith* in order to come into the good of the supernatural things that God offers. In the first verse of 1Corinthians 14 he urges Christians to eagerly (ardently, zealously!) desire to exercise the gifts of the Spirit and especially the gift of prophecy. We have to ask for these tools for Kingdom work, with a living expectation that God *will* give them.

As I write this, I am reminded that on one occasion Jesus said 'From the days of John the Baptist until now, the kingdom of heaven has been forcefully advancing, and forceful ones lay hold of it' (Matt 11:12). Simply being 'open' to the possibility of being used in these ways is not enough! God fills the hungry with good things so that his Kingdom can go forward.

In practice this means that once we have understood enough and come to believe that it is possible for us to prophesy, we need to seek every opportunity to put this gift into practice.

Step 4 - Walk!

Once we *know* the truth, *count* it true of ourselves, and taken the step of faith to *offer* ourselves to exercise one of the gifts of the Holy Spirit, this is where we encounter the mysterious and yet wonderful response of the Holy Spirit. Jesus promises us that he *will* respond when we offer ourselves in these ways to do His will. 'Ask and it will be given to you; seek and you will find; knock and the door will be opened to you. For everyone who asks receives; he who seeks finds; and to him who knocks, the door will be opened.' (Matt 7:7,8)

Here the Lord is encouraging us to actively *offer* ourselves to receive and use his gifts. He goes on to emphasise the goodness of his Father's heart, in that he loves to give his good gifts to his children. 'Which of you, if his son asks for bread, will give him a stone? Or if he asks for a fish, will give him a snake? If you, then, though you are evil, know how to give good gifts to your children, how much more will your Father in heaven give good gifts to those who ask him!' (Matt 7: 9-11) So he is assuring us that provided we are using his gifts for his will and purposes, his Father will give us the supernatural enabling we need for this.

An illustration of these four principles from the Bible

Taking these four steps to do something supernatural like prophesying is perfectly illustrated in a story from Matthew's gospel. In chapter 14:22-36 we are given the story of Jesus walking out on the water in the midst of a major storm to reach His disciples who are struggling to row their boat across the lake.

When they first saw Jesus walking on the lake, we read that they were terrified and cried out 'It's a ghost!'. (A reaction which is not uncommon when Christians are seeking to exercise the gifts of the Spirit in a Church where these supernatural manifestations of the Spirit are still new to most people!) Jesus immediately reassured His disciples 'Take courage! It is I. Don't be afraid.'

Now Peter plainly had the understanding that what Jesus did, his disciples could also do too. Being someone really hungry to grow in the supernatural work of the Kingdom of God, he called out 'Lord, if it's you, tell me to come to you on the water'. Peter had already come to *know* that it was possible for a human being to walk on water in the power of God because he saw Jesus do this. This is why it's vital that as we learn to do supernatural things we not only learn about them from the Scriptures, but see these things modelled by others who may be more mature in this gifting than we are.

Peter was now taking the second step where he was asking the Lord to enable him to *count* this as possible for himself. This is exactly what Jesus went on to do, when he simply said 'Come!'. This is how Peter came to *count* it true that he could walk on water. One day, by the Lord's grace, I would love to meet Peter and ask him

'Peter, what did you feel like just after Jesus said 'Come!'?' Might he then have had some second thoughts as he looked at the ferocity of the storm around them, I wonder?

But then we see a perfect illustration of what it means to *offer* ourselves to do a supernatural thing. Suppose Peter needed to walk from where he had called out to Jesus to another point at the boat in order to be able to climb over the side and down to the water. We need to ask ourselves the very important question 'Did it require any *supernatural* enabling of the Holy Spirit to make it possible for Peter to walk to the side of the boat, or indeed climb down the side of it?'

The answer is plainly 'No!'. Peter had done this countless times, the only difference being that he only did that when the boat docked at the quay side, and he was wanting to come ashore! This time it was to do something only possible in the supernatural enabling of the Spirit. This is what *offering* is. In this stage of the story, Peter was plainly doing what he was doing because he *believed* the Lord's word to him that it was possible for him to walk on water. So *offering* often (if not usually!) means making ourselves vulnerable, having to take a risk of faith as we step out to do something supernatural. And we do feel vulnerable because if the gift does not then come, as Peter must have feared too, we might end up in the water!

It is my personal belief that the water was only hard enough to bear Peter's weight at the moment at which he (by faith!) put his foot on it. God's gifts and his power are usually only released at the *end point* of our faith obedience. God has an important purpose in this, because this in itself is one way in which we bear testimony to our trust in the Lord, because people around us realise that we are only doing what we are doing because we trust his character and promises.

Once he was on the water we see Peter literally *'walking in the Spirit'*, the fourth of Paul's words that we have seen in Romans.

There is another very important lesson we can take out of this story. For as long as Peter kept looking to Jesus as he walked on the water, he was enabled to continue to walk in this supernatural gift. Now the gifts of the Spirit come from the Holy Spirit *through our human spirits*, which once we are born of the Spirit, are in communion with the Holy Spirit. We are spirit, mind (soul) and body as one psychosomatic whole, and the New Testament shows us that our minds and bodies need to be brought into submission to what the Spirit desires.

As Peter continued to walk on the water, his mind must have wandered and started looking at the size of the waves approaching him. I imagine an inner conversation between his mind and his spirit which went something like this: 'Peter, have you seen the size of those waves approaching us right now? And by the way, don't you realise that fishermen normally stay inside boats rather than outside them when they are on the water!' The moment Peter took the focus of his spirit off Jesus and started listening to what his *mind* was saying to him, his faith was quenched and he started to sink.

We need to realise that fear is a powerful, negative form of faith. We only experience fear if we truly *believe* that something bad may be about to happen to us. This negative faith quickly quenches any faith within us that allows the Holy Spirit to do supernatural things through us. This is another reason why it is vital that Church leaders who are wanting to encourage their people to exercise spiritual gifts take real care to put first people at their ease. This then creates an environment where it is safe and easy for people to try new things without fear of failure.

It is also lovely to see how Jesus responded to Peter's loss of faith. Matthew tells us that he *immediately* reached out to Peter and caught him (probably even before he got to knee depth!) and said 'You of little faith, why did you doubt?' My hunch is that the Lord then stood Peter back firmly on the water, perhaps even put an arm around his shoulders, and walked back with him to the boat. And I also believe that far from being unhappy with Peter's 'failure', the Lord was thrilled that he had been so bold as to try to do this supernatural thing. What about the others who were standing in the boat with their knees knocking?

Please read this story carefully for yourself, to see again how the four key words, *(know, count, offer, walk)* that Paul uses in Romans 6-8 were practised by Peter. Ask the Holy Spirit to burn these steps into your memory and heart, and then resolve to put them into practice in practical ways as you seek to grow in the exercise of the gifts of the Holy Spirit, and especially in using the gift of prophecy.

CHAPTER NINE

THREE PRACTICAL LEARNING EXERCISES

Method 1

Described below is a method I have used many times and in many places to help literally thousands of Christians to learn to use the gift of prophecy.

1. Form a group, or groups, of four (maximum five) people, preferably people who do not know one another well. (When you know someone well it is much harder to separate what you think the Lord has shown you from knowledge gleaned by natural means).

2. Tell group members that they won't be put under any duress to have to give prophetic words to the others in their group, but that they must be willing to receive them from the others. They must also be willing to commit themselves to being present for the entire length of the exercise.

3. Set boundaries on what revelation may be received and passed on in this exercise. (No corrective or disciplinary words, prophecies of marriages, pregnancies, impending disasters etc!)

4. First pray for all present, asking that the Lord will fill all afresh with his Spirit, release gifts of prophecy to encourage and bless all present, and that he will not allow the evil one to distort or abuse this ministry.

5. Then explain the procedure that is to be followed, and if there is more than one group, insist that each group keeps in step with your directions so that they all proceed at the same pace. (If they don't, chaos can easily develop!).

The procedure is :-

• Ask the group(s) to choose and focus on one member.

• Ask them to first lay hands on that person, asking the Holy Spirit to come upon him or her, and to release prophetic gifts to the group.

• Tell them to then wait on the Lord in complete silence for at least two minutes, inwardly asking him questions like - 'Lord, how have you gifted this person?' 'What ministry do you want them to exercise now?' 'Is there anything for which you want to commend or praise them?' (e.g. faithfulness in difficult circumstances, integrity in their dealings with people, etc or 'Is there something new that you want to lead this person into?').

• Tell them to use some of this time looking at the person (see earlier section on how God speaks through outward things that we see), and then close their eyes so that they can receive a picture (vision) 'in their mind's eye', or a thought about the person that might come more readily to them if their eyes are closed. (I prefer keeping my eyes open - some spend most of this time with their eyes tight shut! Try both ways.).

• Some might find it helpful to have a notepad on which they can jot things down as they come to them to be held until it is their turn to speak of what they feel they have received.

• After two minutes, tell the others that you are giving them 6 minutes in which to share what they believe the Lord has given them for their chosen person. (Up to 8 minutes can be given for this if the time is available, but a longer time makes the whole exercise too lengthy in most circumstances).

• One person in the group should keep very brief written notes of what has been said on a separate sheet of paper that can be given afterwards to the recipient of the prophecies so that they don't have to memorise all that has been said. Warn them not to get into discussion of what has been spoken, and after they have shared what has come to them, encourage them to continue to ask the Lord for further revelation while others may be speaking.

• When the 6 (or 8) minutes' sharing time is up, ask the group to spend a brief time (one minute or so) praying for their chosen person, thanking the Lord for the things he seems to have spoken, asking him to clarify or confirm some of what has been said, and to bring to fruition those things which may have spoken about the person's future life and ministry.

• The group should then repeat this process - following the lead given - for each of the other three group members.

6. At the very end the leader should thank the Lord for the good gifts he has given, and ask that any words which may not have been from him might fall to the ground and not prove to be a stumbling block for anyone involved in the exercise.

7. It is also helpful to carry out a group testimony exercise at this point. I usually ask everyone present to be utterly honest with themselves and one another in raising their hands only if they can answer yes to the following questions: -

• Did you experience the Lord's love for you through the ministry you received in your group?

• Could you honestly say that you have been comforted, strengthened or encouraged because you believe you have experienced the Lord speaking to you through this exercise?

• How many present could say that they are truly amazed at something that was spoken to them? (i.e. - it just *had* to be God because no-one could have known naturally about what was spoken of, etc). Every time I see this exercise done, some hands go up in answer to this question!

• Were any people *scared* at the outset of this exercise? - Particularly that they wouldn't receive any prophetic gifts at all? (Many hands usually go up at this question!)

• But were any surprised (and delighted!) that the Lord seemed to have used *them* to give a genuine and helpful prophetic gift to another member of their group? (I always love to see the number who put up their hands at this point. These are usually those who have started to use prophecy for the first time.).

• I also like to ask each group present to point out any who seemed to flow in the gift of prophecy with especial ease and accuracy. This might be an early indication of someone who the Lord may be marking out with a call to grow in a prophetic *ministry* within the Church. I then ask the others to pray for these people, asking the Lord to cultivate their gifting and possible prophetic ministry to be a blessing to others and their Churches.

This method is my usual preferred way of releasing Christians in the gift of prophecy. It usually takes about 45 - 60 minutes to carry out.

Provided the teaching has been clear beforehand, and a 'safe' and relaxed environment has been created, it is a joy to then see how readily the Lord gives wonderful gifts through people, even those who are totally new to doing this. I have used it among very conservative folk in country Churches as well as in Churches that already have a lively charismatic tradition. Try it!

Method 2

If people are very hesitant or too shy to try Method 1, here is another way:-

1. Ask people to pair up with one other person, preferably someone they don't know very well.

2. Invite them to pray in silence for one another with no prior discussion, and suggest that in this quiet, each asks the Lord what they should pray for the other.

3. Tell them to pray this in silence, and only afterwards share with one another what they felt they were led to pray for.

Sometimes people are then mutually astonished at how accurately the other's particular needs were revealed by the Holy Spirit.

This exercise can also be done in groups of three or four, but then it would be wise for the focus of prayer to be on one person in the group at a time.

Method 3

After teaching on prophecy (and modelling how personal prophetic words can be given to members of a congregation), the leader should ask the Lord to point out to them two or three of those present who he would like to encourage or speak to, and who would not be unhappy about coming forward and having others present ask the Lord for prophetic words for them.

1. Invite these people to the front, and tell the congregation that they should ask the Lord to point out just one of them to them, and then in the silence provided (at least 2-3 minutes) ask him to give them prophetic words for that person. (It is very important that guidelines are given here about what kind of prophecies are 'off-limits' in an exercise like this! - See Method 1, paragraph 3).

2. Then invite those with prophetic words for one of those up front to speak them out. Ideally these should be tape-recorded or written down in note form.

3. Don't allow any discussion of these words at this point, and be ready to handle any insensitive words that someone might speak in this kind of situation. (e.g. Say 'I really think we need to hold that one' where you feel a real sense of unease about anything that is said. This allows others present to relax, knowing that the process is being responsibly handled.)

4. Once all the words have been spoken for the first person up front, gather them up, emphasising the degree of consistency between

things that have been said, and asking the recipient to comment as well. This sometimes results in gasps of amazement when the congregation realises that the Lord has been giving clear revelation to someone with no natural knowledge of the person up front.

5. It is also important to be aware that the Holy Spirit may come powerfully upon the person receiving prophecies. This often occurs, and the person concerned may need further ministry from a ministry team member present. (It is vitally important that the dignity of those receiving prophecies is protected, so ask the Lord for his wisdom in handling situations that may very occasionally arise.)

6. Then move on to the next person up front and repeat the process.

All these methods have their merits, but as mentioned above, I find Method 1 the best of them all, and it is usually worth encouraging people to try it, provided there is enough time available.

CHAPTER TEN

WEIGHING PROPHECY

Some preliminary comments

The Bible tells us we must weigh prophecy. (1Cor 14:29-32) Unfortunately Paul didn't give us clear instructions about how to do this! But when seeking to weigh a prophecy, we need to ask these basic questions -

Where does it come from?

People can speak out of their own hearts and motives, or by the Holy Spirit (or sometimes a mixture of both!), or even under the influence of a demonic spirit.

When Jesus told Peter that he was going up to Jerusalem, and would be handed over to the authorities to be condemned and crucified, Peter took him aside and began to rebuke him. We then read that Jesus said 'Get behind me, Satan! You do not have in mind the things of God, but the things of men.' It is inconceivable that Jesus would have addressed Peter as Satan! Here the Lord recognised who was actually speaking through Peter as this point. Peter had given Satan opportunity to do so because he was not willing to surrender his own ideas and agenda to God.

This is why the gift of discernment of spirits is so useful in weighing prophecy.

What fruit does it produce, now, or in the fullness of time?

Most prophecies can be weighed immediately they are given. But some relate to what God may be saying about the future, and may have to be stored up in our hearts and weighed only later when it is appropriate to see whether the prophecy has been fulfilled.

In Chapter 5 I wrote of the three dimensions of a prophecy. (The *revelation* itself, the *interpretation* of its meaning, and its *application*). These dimensions must be borne in mind when weighing prophecies, because as mentioned earlier, someone may have received accurate revelation, but has misinterpreted its meaning or mistaken its application.

Six ways to test prophecy

As with much of our teaching in New Wine, what follows owes much to the teaching of John Wimber. He taught that prophecies need to be weighed as follows -

1. Test the content of the prophecy

Ask these questions -

What is being said? When urging Christians not to treat prophecies with contempt, Paul then urges them to 'Test everything. Hold onto the good.' In other words, don't hesitate to strain out or ignore the parts that are not beneficial. (1 Thess 5:19-22)

Is the prophecy confirming something God has already been speaking about? Or is it already being fulfilled in the Church? Ask also - Is God speaking the same things to others in the fellowship? Quite often I have found that when the Lord is speaking about something new, he speaks similar things to several people in a short space of time. I love this!

Is the prophecy consistent with what the Bible teaches about the Lord? Does it connect us to Him, and reveal him and his nature as the Bible reveals him?

2. Test the prophecy against Scripture

Prophecy often focuses attention on Scripture. It can draw people back to a key truth that they have been ignoring. Or it gives us an enhanced understanding of what the Bible teaches.

In the early 1990's there was a prophecy given that said 'Seek my face and not my hands.' People were getting more excited about obtaining revelation from the Lord about what he might want to do with them, than they were in coming to the Lord for his own sake in personal worship and prayer. This prophecy is fully consistent with the teaching of the Bible. A careful study of Ezekiel 44:10-14 shows this all too clearly! (I commend this passage to any busy Christian). **Prophecy does NOT add to Scripture, or conflict with it.** (Rev 22:18-19) This is always true, because of the inspired nature of the Bible. However, we must be very careful not to be too hasty in throwing out something in a prophecy because it doesn't seem to agree with our understanding of Scripture, or our theology or doctrinal stance. God warns us in Isaiah that his thoughts are far, far higher than ours, and that his ways are not our ways. (Isaiah 55:8,9) In the context of renewing his people, he also warns that he will lead his 'blind' servants by ways they have not known, and along unfamiliar paths. (Isa 42:16,18-20).

For example, suppose a bachelor in your Church one day announced that he believed that the Lord had told him to marry someone who was known to be a prostitute? (I am glad I have not had to face this situation as a pastor!) But this is precisely what God told Hosea to do! (Hos 1:2 - 'Go, take to yourself an adulterous wife....!') Perhaps this kind of situation might now never arise, but we are nevertheless in danger of confusing our own appreciation of the Bible with what it actually reveals to us about the Lord.

So this is a warning that we should not be over-hasty in our process of weighing some prophecies, especially if they come through someone with a mature prophetic ministry.

3. Test the prophecy by determining its fruit

Ask questions like -

• Has the prophecy been beneficial to the fellowship?

• Is this evident with the passage of time?

• What has been the result, or effect of the prophecy?

4. Test the spirit of the prophecy

Does the prophecy bring conviction - or condemnation? (Jn 10:2-5) From what Paul teaches in 1Cor 14:3, does it bring -

Edification? Paul here used the Greek word 'oikodome' which means to build up, as in building a house (oikos) with good, strong materials. So ask - 'Does it strengthen us in our standing in the Lord?'

Encouragement? The Greek word here is 'paraklesis' from which one name for the Holy Spirit, 'Paraclete', comes. Does it build and release faith? I have given examples in Chapter 2 of prophecies that brought much encouragement and fresh faith to people.

Comfort/consolation? This Greek word is 'paramythia' - the solace afforded by love. (See Phil 2:1) When we are really under pressure, perhaps facing resistance or obstacles when seeking to do what the Lord has spoken to us, prophecies can calm our fears and doubts, and help us to rest in the Lord.

5. Test the prophet

In the 1960's and 1970's we were taught 'Weigh the prophecy, not the prophet.' In other words, we should avoid bringing our knowledge of the person's character and spirituality to bear as a factor in weighing a prophecy they give. This is not strictly a Biblical idea!

For others who prophesy to us - Jesus taught that we should beware of prophetic people who come to us as 'wolves in sheep's clothing.' (Matt 7:15-23) He taught us that 'good trees bear good fruit, and bad trees bear bad fruit.' (Lk 6:43-45) In effect he is plainly saying 'Take a hard look at the person prophesying!'

Ask questions like -

• Do they prophesy according to the measure of their faith? Or has spiritual excitement taken them out of their depth? (Rom 12:6)

• Do they revere and love the Lord? Does he excite them more than exercising their gifting?

• Are they hungering to become pure in heart, holy, with their lives conformed to the whole counsel of Scripture?

• Are they growing in spiritual maturity - or falling back?

• How do they respond to correction? Are they teachable?

BUT! If we are going to mature and grow prophetic people in the fellowship, we must give them room to grow and make mistakes! We only 'prophesy in part' anyway! We must also be very gentle with them! (Remember that prophetic people commonly have a history of rejection in their lives.)

For ourselves as we seek to grow in prophetic gifting - There is always the danger that prophetic people will seek to find their identity in their gifting. So as we seek to grow in prophecy, we need to ask ourselves questions like these -

• Do I leave, or want to leave a meeting if the leader questions or rejects the revelation I bring?

• Do I preface my prophecies with 'The Lord told me', making it much harder for others to openly question whether my prophecy really was from the Lord?

• What is my true motive for sharing what I receive from the Lord?

• Do I have a need to be right all the time?

• Do I often imply that I know more than I do - in a mysterious way?

• Do I try to present myself as spiritually unique? (Dress, actions, manner of speech, name dropping ... ?)

• Do I often try to pass off my moods/actions as being the 'burden of the Lord'?

• Do I tell everything I perceive to be from God - to anyone who will listen?

If the answer to any of these questions is yes, we need to face reality! We need to become more honest with ourselves, sharing *ourselves* as we *really are* with others, repenting of past wrong patterns of behaviour with our gifting, asking for help, and making ourselves accountable to others.

6. *In conclusion*

Use these questions as an overall test of prophecies -

• Do they lead me to Christ, or do they direct me somewhere, or to someone else?

• Do they exalt Jesus in all His glory and majesty?

• Do they lead me to love Him even more than I did before?

Or -

• Do they lead me away from the simplicity of single-hearted devotion to Him?

And test all prophecies with sincerity, love and a gracious heart.

CHAPTER 11

CULTIVATING PROPHECY IN THE LOCAL CHURCH

SOME POINTERS FOR LEADERS

Because things can easily go wrong with prophecy, leaders need to be especially alert to deal with problems promptly and firmly - albeit with love and gentleness! For example, leaders need to be aware of the particular temptations that come to people with a genuine prophetic gifting, and they must also be wise in the way they seek to evolve and develop the expression of gifts of prophecy in Church meetings and public services.

Temptations prophetic people face

1. Abusing prophecy to seek to impress others. I find that it is very easy to fall for this temptation, especially if prophetic people have been asked to give personal words openly for people at a congregational or conference meeting. Our desire to please people can make it all too easy to want to bestow greater blessings, or speak about a greater giftedness to someone we speak to in the Lord's name than he might himself be saying to that person.

2. Abusing prophecy to gain influence or even control over others' lives. Beware the prophetic person who seems to encourage people to keep coming back to them to give them the 'word of the Lord' for their lives. As mentioned earlier, the fruit of true prophetic ministry must always be that the Lord's role in a person's life increases, and that of the prophet decreases. Those with recognised prophetic gifting in a Church need to be taught not to allow others to use them in this way. ('You're a man/woman of God - seek the word of the Lord for me.' In other words 'I'm abdicating my own responsibility to seek the Lord to you.') Teach them to tell these people that they should *seek the Lord for themselves*, ask others to pray for God's guidance for them, and *privately* ask the Lord to help them by moving someone in the fellowship to come to them with an unsolicited word.

3. Refusing to allow their words to be weighed by others. Despite the clear teaching of the Bible about weighing prophecy (see Chapter 9), sadly some people who may have a proven gifting may come to assume a measure of infallibility. This is usually aggravated if they suffer from low self-esteem, where to be shown to be wrong would be taken very personally. These people need very careful, loving handling, but they must not be allowed to exercise their prophetic gifting if they will not submit their prophecies to be weighed by others, or accept pastoring from a leader in the Church (who may not necessarily be as prophetically gifted as they are!). Dealing with people like these can be very painful indeed, and the leader concerned feels very vulnerable to the accusation that can sometimes be spoken or at least implied that they are resisting the Holy Spirit. But leaders must be courageous, because otherwise problems like these can cause terrible damage and hindrance to the development of prophecy in the Church.

4. Confusing responsibility for delivering a prophetic word with leadership authority to ensure that it is responded to. This error can cause havoc in Churches, and quickly destroy spiritual unity. Sometimes immature and rather headstrong Christians (who do have a genuine and perhaps even very significant prophetic gifting) get very agitated if their Church leaders don't appear to be heeding or responding to a word that they have delivered to them. They feel that they remain responsible for 'making' the Church leaders respond, because God had chosen to speak this word through them. These people need to be taught that once they have faithfully (and humbly!) delivered their word to the leaders, their responsibility is fully discharged. And as mentioned in an earlier chapter, if they feel that the leaders are not making an adequate response, the most powerful thing they can do is to take the matter up with the Lord in private prayer, first sincerely asking his blessing for the leaders, and then asking him to get them to take heed of what he was saying to them. Following this course of action preserves 'the unity of the Spirit in the bond of peace' (Eph 4:3). Going round talking to others in the Church expressing their concern that their leaders were being 'disobedient' to the Lord most certainly does not!

5. Isolating themselves when their prophetic words don't appear to be received. This is another way prophetically gifted Christians can respond to correction, and it is symptomatic of the extent to which they seek to find their identity in their gifting. ('If you don't receive my gift, you are rejecting me too.')

6. Claiming a prophetic authority they don't have. Watch out for those who portray everything they say or do as if it came directly from God - this is just another form of (super spiritual!) self-righteousness.

Cultivating prophecy in open meetings

If a Church is new to the idea of prophetic gifts being expressed at its gatherings, then leaders need to be very careful in the way prophetic ministry is developed. I would encourage them to consider the following steps :

1. Teach about it to the whole Church, showing how the Bible urges the Church to eagerly desire the expression of this gift, and the development of prophetic ministries.

2. Consider holding an open mid-week meeting to which all are invited. Let people opt out, rather than be seen to be choosing your own 'keen' Christians. Invite a competent outside teacher to come with a team of responsible prophetic ministers to teach and model the exercise of prophetic gifts. Modelling is key here. Many Christians find it easy to have their opinions about whether prophecy is available today, or what forms it should take, but I have seen many change their views very quickly once they have had first-hand experience of the blessing and help the Lord can give through prophecies! (Sometimes when we have gone too visit Churches that are very nervous about prophecy, we have asked that our first evening is with their eldership or leadership team. The Lord seems to know exactly who most needs to be persuaded and has given very significant words either for them or their spouse! This has then opened a big door for prophecy into the Church itself.).

3. After the meeting that is open to all, invite all those who would like to grow further in prophecy to come to a series of regular meetings for more teaching about it, or hold a Saturday teaching day. Look out for those who are not only clearly gifted, but also seem fairly mature in the way they handle their gifting. (See Chapter 3), and find a way to further encourage and train them. Then give them

authority to exercise their gifting, setting appropriate boundaries for its expression (e.g. - only in the mid-week meeting, or in their Home Group, or at the Sunday evening services etc).

4. Develop the regular expression and weighing of prophetic words in an informal Church meeting (weekly prayer meetings are often the best - see Chapter 2) where those present are happy to accept that people are learning to step out in new ways in the gifts of the Holy Spirit, and are tolerant of others getting it wrong. This provides a safe place to learn and grow, and those leading these meetings the opportunity to grow in experience in handling some of the situations that can arise. (There is no substitute for experience!) So I would urge that the Sunday morning service should NOT be the first place to launch the Church out in prophecy!

5. But leaders should also regularly encourage their people to bring them prophetic words for the Church or themselves, preferably written down. Where appropriate, the leader might either include the prophecy in a sermon, or at some other suitable point in a Sunday service. Or the person who first received it could be encouraged to give out the word themselves.

6. See also the comments in Chapter 10 about what to do when weighing particular prophecies.

IN CONCLUSION...

Prophecy is a precious and powerful gift of God, which he loves to give to bless, guide and encourage his people.

It requires active faith to grow and persevere in exercising it, and as with other gifts of the Spirit, its use in the Church will grow or die according to the priority we give it in our gatherings. Again and again we need to return to the place in which we seek the Lord with child-like trust and expectancy, rejoicing in how much he loves us and others around us, and speaking out what he reveals to us.

May the Lord strengthen you with his Spirit, and make you very wise and fruitful in your use of this beautiful gift.

New Wine Vision and Core Values

Vision
To equip and encourage churches throughout the nation to reach their communities with the gospel of Jesus Christ and his Kingdom, by being continuously renewed by the Holy Spirit.

Core values
Local Church life that is welcoming, relational, accessible for all generations, and builds community and family life.

Intimate Worship that is accessible, passionate, joyful, inspiring, culturally appropriate and facilitates encounter with God.

Anointed Leadership that is visionary, courageous, humble, consistent, full of faith, and releases church members into their God-given ministries.

Strategic Mission that is holistic, inspired and empowered by the Spirit, concerned with justice and care for the poor, and encourages new church planting initiatives.

Orthodox Theology with doctrine and morality founded on the Bible and the person, teaching and work of Jesus Christ.

Bible-based Teaching and training that is interesting, thoughtful, and equipping for everyday life and ministry.

Committed Discipleship that models Christian love, prayerfulness, holiness, integrity, accountability, humility and generosity, and enables us to serve like Jesus.

Every member ministry that is gift-orientated, life transforming and expresses God's love and power.

* These values are in no particular order of priority

New Wine, 4a Ridley Avenue, Ealing, London W13 9XW, England
Tel: 020 8567 6717 www.new-wine.org

New Wine International, c/o Christ Church Roxeth, Roxeth Hill, Harrow, Middlesex, HA2 0JN
Tel: 020 8864 2965 www.new-wine.org